Advanced Principles of Prediction

Advanced Principles of Prediction

GAYATRI DEVI VASUDEV

MOTILAL BANARSIDASS
INTERNATIONAL
DELHI

Reprint Edition : Delhi, 2025
First Edition : 2002

© Author

ISBN : 978-93-48128-47-8 (PB)
ISBN : 978-93-48128-02-7 (HB)

Also available at
MOTILAL BANARSIDASS INTERNATIONAL
H.O. : 41 U.A. Bungalow Road, (Back Lane)Jawahar Nagar, Delhi - 110 007
4261 (basement) Lane #3,Ansari Road, Darya Ganj, New Delhi - 110 002
Shop No. 6, Luz Ginza Complex, 241 Luz Corner, Mylapore, Chennai - 600 004
12/1A, 2nd Floor, Bankim Chatterjee Street, Kolkata - 700 073
Stockist : Motilal Books, Ashok Rajpath, Near Kali Mandir, Patna - 800 004

No part of this book may be reproduced in any form or by any electronic or mechanical means including information storage and retrieval systems without permission in writing from the publishers, excepts by a reviewer who may quote brief passages in a review.

Printed in India
MOTILAL BANARSIDASS INTERNATIONAL

To
my beloved parents
Dr. B.V. Raman and Mrs. Rajeswari Raman
and the unconditional love they have given me

Introduction

Interest is astrology has been growing as never before in recent times, especially over the last few decades. A big contribution to this were the life-long efforts of my revered father Dr. B.V. Raman to create intelligent interest in the subject amongst the educated public. Towards this end, Dr. Raman wrote several books dealing with almost every aspect of both computational as well as predictive astrology. These books not only introduce the science to the student but also take one into the different nuances of astrology. Seen against this background, the present book is an attempt to take the student through a slightly different area of the predictive principles of astrology not hitherto dealt with. Concepts such as *Badhaka*, *Kendradhipati Dosha*, *Gulika* and *Mandi*, *Ayurveda* and others are found in almost all classical works of astrology where they are clearly defined; but the studnet is often bewildered by seeming contradictions when the question of their application to actual charts comes up.

Jupiter is described as the most powerful benefic according to general principles of interpretation. On the other hand, the *Badhaka* theory makes out Jupiter to be an incorrigible malefic for certain ascendants. How does one reconcile such diametrically opposing properties of planets? Actual case studies in may experience have thrown up clues that help to deal with all such ambiguities and contradictions that one comes across when taking up a chart for interpretation.

Kendradhipati is another little understood concept. Under certain conditions, it becomes extremely powerful for evil and at other times, it ceases to cause the havoc normally associated with it. This is, more or less, dependent upon where such a *kendra* lord is placed and leads to different kinds of results under different planetary circumstances.

Dustanas, as the name implies, are often treated with fear and as causing harm. But what kind of harm each *Dustana* can cause and how far, as also how it can also not be harmful, depends on several factors in the horoscope.

Remedial measures are a concomitant of astrology, and the wide and complex range of such measures available can be bewildering. Many a time, simple measures performed with earnestness can prove highly efficacious in handling horoscopic afflictions. I have tried to approach this part of astrology in as direct and simple a manner as possible.

Muhurtha is a section of astrology on which several classical authorities have written exhaustively. *Prasna* or horary astrology is also a section of the subject to which recourse is taken on many occasions for solutions to problems. I have tried a novel approach trying to use a *Muhurtha* chart as a *Prasna* chart with good results. My effort contains only the germ of an idea in this direction. I am sure readers will examine and investigate this approach critically for what it is worth.

Gulika and *Mandi* have been the subject of endless discussion — whether they are the same entity or quite different ones. *Gulika is often treated as totally* destructive of the significance of the house he occupies by some; others hold the house he aspects gets damaged instead. These are extreme views and I have tried a more moderate approach to interpret the nature of results of which *Gulika* is capable of.

Ayurdaya or the judgement of longevity is a complex and baffling topic. Whole tomes can be written on it but I have confined myself to juding longevity in a general sense as relevant to situations one constantly meets with in life and where major decisions are to be made. Such an approach to longevity, though not detailed enough to specify the exact date of death, can be an invaluable guide to planning one's life.

I have tried to present these advanced principles in as simple a manner as the topic will allow without straying beyond the parameters set by classical authorities on the subject.

The conclusions I have arrived at with regard to the concepts I have dealt with in these pages are based on the study of countless charts; yet I do not claim mine to be the last word on them. Nevertheless, if a study of this book can help a student of astrology to gain a little more insight than existing works on the subject allow, I would have the satisfaction that my efforts have been amply rewarded. The contents of the volume have earlier appeared in *The Astrological Magazine.*

The science of astrology is like an ocean and my work, I believe, is an honest attempt at trying to analyse just one tiny drop in the endless waves of this vast body of knowledge.

I thank Mr. Chawla, Mr. Balram Sadhwani and Mr. Vivek Ahuja of UBS Publishers' Distributors Ltd. for publishing the book elegantly. I also express my gratefulness to Mr. Niranjan Babu, C.E.O. and Publisher, *The Astrological Magazine,* for his suggestions and assistance in the production of the book. My grateful thanks also go to Mr. Gopinath, Mr. Sanjeeva Rao and Mrs. Mahalakshmi who have helped me at vairous stages of the production of this volume.

Gayatri Devi Vasudev

Contents

	Introduction	vii
1.	The Badhaka as a Supplementary Tool	1
2.	Kendradhipati Dosha — A Selective Affliction	13
3.	A Critical Examination of Dustanas	33
4.	Enemies from the Sixth House	47
5.	The Eighth House and Calamities	59
6.	Miscellaneous Matters from Dustanas	69
7.	Good and Bad Results from Dustanas	79
8.	Understanding Rahu and Ketu	87
9.	Planets and Palliatives	101
10.	Notes on Gulika and Mandi	115
11.	More Notes on Gulika and Mandi	127
12.	Combining Different Dasa Systems — Right or Wrong?	143
13.	The Fallacy of Combining Different Dasa Systems	155
14.	Muhurtha, Prasna and Political Predictions	165
15.	Planets and Underground Water Sources	179
16.	Judging Ayurdaya — Some Broad Guidelines	195
17.	Judging Ayurdaya — More Guidelines	207
18.	Ayurdaya and Crucial Decisions	221

Chapter 1

The Badhaka
as a Supplementary Tool

Chapter 1

The Earthworm
as a Supplementary Food

1

THE FIRST step in understanding the much feared but little used concept of Badhaka is to start with the definitions.

What are the Badhaka planets or Badhaka signs ? They are said to be the 11th, the 9th and the 7th signs (or their lords or planets in them) from the Ascendant for moveable (Chara), fixed (Sthira) and common (Dwiswabhava) signs respectively. This is a rather incomplete definition, for were it to be effective, every other chart would be under a state of perpetual torment. For, Badhaka literally means tormentor. The complete definition is given in **Jataka Parijata** (Chapter II, Sloka 48) :

क्रमाच्चरागद्विशरीरभानामुपान्त्यधर्मस्मरगास्तदीश: ।
खरेशमान्दिस्थितराशिनाथा ह्यतीव बाधकरस्वेचरा: स्यु: ॥ ४८ ॥

meaning, *in the case of moveable, immoveable and dual signs, planets occupying respectively the 11th, 9th or 7th from them or their lords will prove exceedingly troublesome if they happen to own at the same time the houses occupied by the lord of Khara or Mandi.*

Therefore, in order for a planet to qualify as a Badhaka two conditions are laid down.

Firstly, the 11th, the 9th and the 7th houses or their lords or planets in them for moveable, fixed and common signs respectively can be considered.

Secondly, such a planet should simultaneously be the ruler of the house occupied by Kharesha or Mandi.

Mandi is a commonly known factor. What about Kharesha ?

Khara is defined in Sloka 56, Chapter V of **Jataka Parijata** :

विलग्नजन्मद्रेक्काणाद्यस्तु द्वाविंशतिः खरः ।

Khara is the 22nd Drekanna from the Ascendant. Its ruler is the Kharesha.

Therefore, a planet can become a Badhaka under only certain circumstances. That implies many charts may not have a Badhaka at all. This makes sense, for the 11th, 9th and 7th houses often give very good results belying the nomenclature Badha itself.

What results can a Badhaka specifically point to ? According to Sloka 30, Chapter XVIII of the same classical text :

बाधास्थानपतद्युतग्रहदशा शोकादिरोगप्रदा
तत्केन्द्रस्थदशापहारसमये दुःखं विदेशाटनम् ।

The Dasa period of a planet owning a Badhakastana (as well as of the one associated with it) leads to disease, distress and other such evils. During the Dasa and Bhukti of a planet occupying a Kendra from the Badhakastana, sorrow and foreign travel will be experienced.

In **Prasna Marga**, a different definition is given which can lead to some confusion. The Arudha Lagna is taken as the centre of the chart to define Badhaka as the ruler of the 11th, 9th or 7th house with reference to the Arudha sign being moveable, fixed or common respectively and the definition stops at this point. There is no mention of Khara or Mandi although the views of other scholars on slight variations of the definitions are given by the author. This simplified definition of **Prasna Marga** is generally applicable to Prasna charts; for elsewhere in Chapter 2, Sloka 6, the author quotes Vasishta as saying "Those who desire to know the future, whether they ask or not, deserve to be given predictions on the basis of Arudha" at the time of Prasna. Thereafter, the author instructs the astrologer to make a proper note of the exact time, omens, gesticulations etc., of the querent. The emphasis on noting question time correctly implies the Prasna chart.

Prasna Marga also mentions 2 more definitions. The quadrants from the Badhakas it defines can also be Badhakas.

The third definition is less general and puts Aquarius as the Badhaka for all moveable signs, that is, for Aries, Cancer, Libra and Capricorn.

Scorpio is the house of harm for Leo, Virgo, Scorpio and Sagittarius.

Taurus has Capricorn as a Badhakastana.

Cancer is the house of harm for Aquarius and Sagittarius is the Badhaka for Gemini and Pisces.

The first and third definitions are endorsed by the author of **Prasna Marga**.

It looks as if the role of a Badhaka in Prasna Marga is restricted mainly to problems of the mind, body and soul — mental illness, physical ailments and psychic disturbances. It does not take stock of other kinds of problems like social, family, economic, professional and other. The emphasis here is on tracing the root or source of the misery one is passing through and prescribing appropriate remedial measures. The planets and respective deities are listed alongside of afflictions appropriate to each deity.

The 6th, 8th and 12th houses are known as Dustanas and some writers include them under Badhaka houses. The Dustanas cannot be Badhaka houses and this is made clear in Sloka 31, Chapter XV of **Prasna Marga** when the author says,

जीवः सन्बाधकेशो व्ययमतिरिपुगो यद्गहेः केन्द्रसंस्थः ।

meaning, *If Jupiter as lord of a house (Badhaka) of harm occupies the 6th, 8th or 12th and these happen to be the Kendras of Rahu............*where he makes a clear demarcation between Badhakas and Dustanas.

The Badhaka in the birth chart may affect the significations of the house it occupies or owns or even its natural significations (Karakattwa) causing problems and setbacks of a serious nature. Does a chart without Badhaka sail though life without problems ?

Chart 1 : Born 15-5-1935 at 1-40 a.m. (IST) at 12 N 18, 76 E 37 with a balance of 2 years 11 months 24 days of Moon Dasa at birth.

	SUN 1 MERC. 19	VENUS 12		SAT.	VENUS	MARS	MERC
SAT. 17 ASCDT. 15	Chart 1 Rasi		KETU 4	ASCDT. RAHU	Navamsa		
RAHU 4				SUN			KETU
	MANDI 12	JUPT. (R) 26	MARS 15 MOON 29			MANDI	MOON

The Ascendant in Chart 1 being Aquarius. the 9th house is Libra, its ruler is Venus and its occupant is Jupiter.

The 22nd Drekanna will be the 2nd Drekanna of Virgo which, in turn, falls in Capricorn ruled by Saturn. Saturn is in Aquarius also ruled by himself. The lord of Khara or Kharesha is, therefore, Saturn. Mandi occupies Scorpio ruled by Mars. Since the 9th lord Venus nor the 9th occupant Jupiter is the same as the ruler of Khara or of the sign occupied by Mandi, this horoscope has no Badhaka with reference to Lagna.

Since all classical authorities without exception attribute equal strength to both the Ascendant as well as the Moon-sign, we can also examine the chart from the Moon-sign.

The Moon-sign is Virgo. The 7th house is Pisces and its lord is Jupiter. The 22nd Drekanna from the Moon is the last Drekanna of Aries which falls in Sagittarius. Jupiter is Kharesha. Jupiter occupies Libra ruled by Venus. Mandi is in a sign ruled by Mars. Since the 7th lord is not the same as Venus or Mars, this horoscope does not have a Badhaka from the Moon-sign either.

Yet, the native has had her share of suffering. Belonging to a conservative family with a highly respectable social background, the native was shocked when her son (who did not do well in his studies either) went and married, out of caste, a girl from a very ordinary background. The daughter, a beautiful girl, stunned the native by marrying a restaurant bearer in some Arab country. Even without the Badhaka, these unhappy developments can be traced to basic afflictions in the chart. No doubt Yogakaraka Venus occupies the 5th; but the 5th and its occupant are hemmed between malefics Sun and Ketu. The 5th lord Mercury is in the 12th thereform. Jupiter aspects the 5th house but being retrograde and a malefic, made things go awry.

The Badhaka, which is not present in every chart, can therefore have no decisive role in chart-interpretation. It can be taken only as a supplementary factor.

In Chart 2, the events that interest us center round the 7th house.

Chart 2: Born 9-9-1960 at 7-15 p.m. (IST) at 18 N 56, 72 E 51 with a balance of 14 years 9 months 18 days of Venus Dasa at birth.

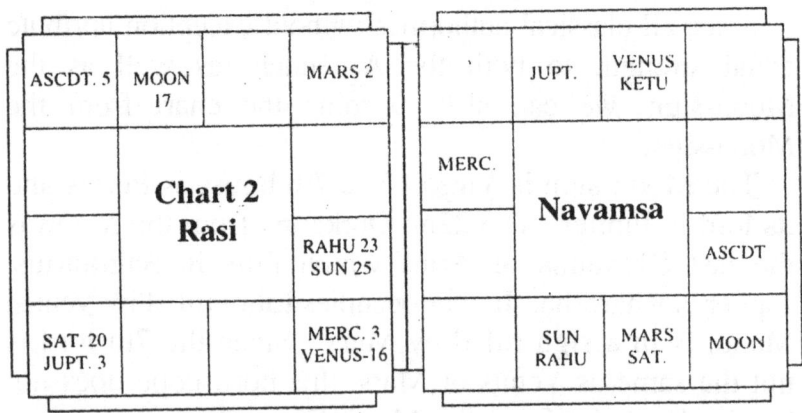

The 7th lord is Mercury in Chart 2. The Ascendant being in the 1st Drekanna of Pisces, the 22nd Drekanna is in the 1st Drekanna of Libra ruled by Venus. Venus, in turn, occupies Virgo ruled by Mercury. Therefore since the 7th lord Mercury (Lagna being common sign) is the same as the lord of Kharesha, Mercury becomes Badhaka. *Prima facie*, the presence of Badhaka in the 7th house seems to have played havoc with the native's marital happiness.

The native's first wife lived with him for 8 years but her addiction to gambling and other vices led to a divorce. The second wife stayed with him for 20 days after which she left him. She too obtained a divorce but on the ground he was impotent. Can we conclude Mercury in the 7th as a full-fledged Badhaka has led to much marital suffering ?

Ignoring Mercury's role as Badhaka, let us take a look at the 7th house using the simple analysis of 7th house factors and Karaka Venus.

The 7th lord Mercury is in the 7th with 8th lord Venus. The sign is a common sign and both the 7th house and its occupants which include Kalatrakaraka Venus are aspected by 11th lord Saturn and 2nd and 9th lord Mars, again from common signs, indicating multiple marriages.

Venus in a dual sign aspected by malefics Mars or Saturn alone can by itself show more than one marriage. Here both the natural malefics aspect Venus involving only common signs adding to the affliction.

Further, as indicated in **Brihat Parasara Hora**, Chapter 19, Sloka 21,

द्विस्वभावगते शुक्रे स्वोच्चे तद्राशिनायके ।
दारेशे बलसंयुक्ते बहुदार समन्वितः ॥

Venus in a dual sign and the ruler of this sign in his exaltation sign and the 7th lord in strength is said to cause a Bahu-dara Yoga (a Yoga for multiple marriages). Here, these planetary positions are literally present. Venus is in Virgo whose ruler Mercury occupies his sign of exaltation. As 7th lord also Mercury is strong. Therefore, without bringing the Badhaka into the picture, the afflictions point to the marital miseries of the native. The Badhaka power (tormenting power) of Mercury may be said to have shown up in the fact the divroce, both times, came under extremely distressing and humiliating circumstances.

The Ascendant in Chart 3 being Sagittarius, the 7th lord is Mercury. The 22nd Drekanna falls in the 3rd Drekanna of Cancer. The ruler of this Drekanna is Jupiter who is the Kharesha. He occupies Gemini ruled by Mercury who is also the 7th lord here. Mercury becomes a Badhaka and aspects the Ascendant, occupies the 7th house and rules the 10th house. The significations of all these houses suffered. As a great patriot and revolutionary, the native, Vinayak Damodar Savarkar, clashed violently with the British jeopardising his career and life. He went through untold suffering for the sake of his country. He was persecuted, arrested, tried and finally convicted and put in prison with fetters on his hands and legs. Jupiter,

Chart 3 : Born 28-5-1883 at 9-25 p.m. (LMT) at 18 N 23, 73 E 53 with a balance of 1 year 1 month 26 days of Mars Dasa at birth.

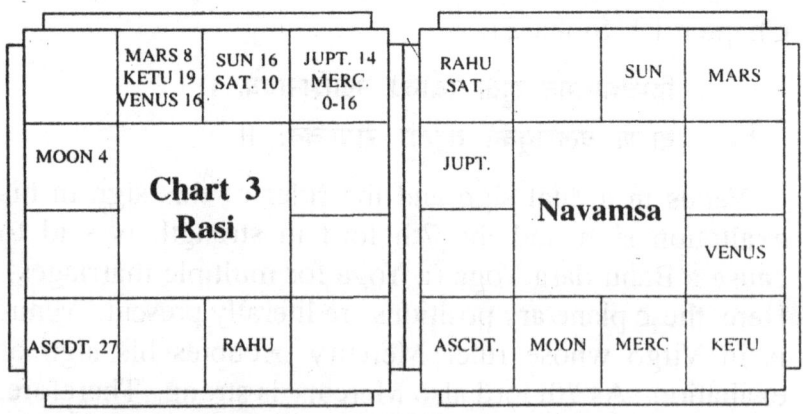

as ruler of the Ascendant, aspecting the Ascendant does not warrant such suffering and privation. However, Jupiter himself is afflicted being in an Ayudha Drekanna and Aridra Nakshatra. Mercury joining him and aspecting Lagna only made the affliction stronger which in turn led the native to sacrifice and forsake his own interests for the sake of the motherland.

What we can surmise from such charts as these is the Badhaka by himself does not generate adverse results. If the chart has basic afflictions and the Badhaka also focuses his influence on them, the afflictions tend to get aggravated.

Every chart need not have a Badhaka. And simply because the Badhaka can be identified in a particular chart does not mean the chart can be condemned outright. The role of a Badhaka is subtle and can only act as a catalyst or abettor of a basic affliction. To that extent, its role is limited and active only under certain circumstances in a birth chart.

In a Prasna chart, however, the Badhaka assumes menacing proportions and can make or mar the chart.

(09-'95)

Chapter 2

Kendradhipati Dosha — A Selective Affliction

2

ALL CLASSICAL WORKS on Jyotisha have a chapter devoted to definitions. Familiarising oneself with these definitions, makes the complex and difficult art of interpretation relatively less strenuous. *Kendradhipati* means lord or ruler of a Kendra or a quadrant. The 1st, the 4th, the 7th and the 10th are defined as Kendras and the rulers of these houses as Kendra lords. The Dosha or affliction associated with the ownership of Kendras is what is known as Kendradhipati Dosha.

केन्द्राधिपतयः सौम्या दिशन्ति नहि सत्फहम् ।
क्रूरा नैवाशुभं कुर्युस्त्रिकोणेशाः शुभाः स्मृताः ॥
— B. P. H. 35-02

According to Parasara, benefics as Kendra lords do not give good results. Likewise, malefics as Kendra lords do not give Asubha or malefic results. But Trikona lords or the rulers of trines, irrespective of their being benefic or malefic, always give good results.

The terms *benefic* and *malefic* used here are with reference to the classification of planets as natural benefics and natural malefics.

Jupiter, Venus, well-associated Mercury and waxing Moon are the natural benefics. The natural malefics are the Sun, Saturn, Mars, afflicted Mercury and waning or weak Moon.

Therefore, **Kendradhipati Dosha** as an affliction attaches itself only to Jupiter, Venus, well-placed Mercury and waxing Moon. The Sun, Mars, Saturn, afflicted Mercury and the weak Moon are immune to this Dosha.

The Parasari Sloka while defining Kendradhipati Dosha lays down three principles of interpretation.

1. Natural benefics as lords of Kendras do not give good results.
2. Natural malefics as lords of Kendras do not give inauspicious results.
3. Trinal lords, irrespective of whether they are natural benefics or malefics, give good results.

The Ascendant is, by definition, both a Kendra and a Trikona and therefore, its ruler, is always a benefic. Extending this definition to planets other than the Ascendant lord, we have the Yogakaraka whose power to do good flows from the same principle that makes the Ascendant lord always benefic. Where a planet owns both a Kendra and a Trikona at the same time, its power to do good overcomes its Kendradhipati Dosha, if it is a natural benefic, giving rise to a Yogakaraka.

The Dasa of a natural benefic owning a Kendra may be deemed inauspicious. Jupiter and Venus as lords of Kendras attract power to cause evil results. If they, at the same time, occupy Maraka houses such as the 2nd and the 7th, their power for evil extends to even causing death, but not necessarily. Such results can include totally unexpected and devastating situations in life as well.

Well-associated Mercury, if he owns a Kendra, is said to be less powerful than Jupiter and Venus in causing adverse results. The Moon is the least effective, as a Kendra lord, in generating bad results.

The affliction arising from owning a Kendra or Kendradhipati Dosha is dealt with, in all classical works, as one of several factors qualifying the power of a planet to give bad results. The very fact it is one of a long list of factors qualifying a planet appears to emphasise the fact that its role in influencing results must necessarily be limited and even selective. This Dosha may be said to blemish the planet in a manner that whatever the benefic or favorable results normally attributed to it may get suspended or even converted into totally unfavorable results.

According to **Jataka Parijata** (II – 73-74),

राहुदोषं बुधो हन्यादुभयोस्तु शनैश्चरः।
याणां भूमिजो हन्ति चतुर्णां दानवार्चितः ॥
पंचानां देवमन्त्री च षण्णां दोषं तु चन्द्रमाः ।
सप्तदोषंरविहन्याद्विशेषादुत्तरायणे ॥

Mercury (when in strenght) is said to counter the evil caused by Rahu. Saturn can counter the evil caused by the combining of Mercury and Rahu. Mars is said to be capable of overcoming the evil generated by these 3 planets put together. Venus can counter the evil caused by all these 4 planets being together. Jupiter can overcome the joint evil of all the 5 planets Mercury, Rahu, Saturn, Mars and Venus. The Sun is said to be so powerful that he can remove the evil effects of the foregoing planets *plus* of the Moon.

These results are attributed to the planets when they are benefics. But should Jupiter, Venus or Mercury or the Moon acquire Kendradhipati Dosha, the power of each of these planets to hem in the evil caused by the others gets affected. At such times, malefic results attributed to these planets may get a free hand to run amok.

Jupiter is associated with knowledge and happiness and when he gets Kendradhipati Dosha, these significations are adversely hit.

Venus is said to rule desire and love and conjugal life and as a Kendra lord can make life deficient in these areas.

Mercury rules speech and communication skills and if he acquires Kendradhipati Dosha, one has trouble in these abilities.

The Moon is said to rule the mind of the Kalapurusha and if he is afflicted by owning a Kendra, mental peace and health become a casualty.

Other results that the natural benefics as Kendra lords can generate are :

The Moon : Trouble through diseases and ailments brought about by a reckless and promiscuous life style, nasal problems, jaundice, hallucinations, delusion and obsessive complexes.

Mercury : Gastric trouble, digestive and stomach problems, leprosy, indigestion, colic, diarrhoea, stammering, skin ailments, speech difficulty, mental retardation, nervous disorders, academic frustration.

Venus : Diseases springing from wayward carnal pleasures, excessive drinking, diabetes, conjugal misery and even cruelty from marital partner as well as a vain search and craving for love that may never be found.

Jupiter : Lack of mental peace, childlessness, mentally retarded or physically handicapped children, the ire of pious people, vulnerability to witchcraft and black magic, loss of status, reputation and honour and prestige.

The natural benefics become Kendradhipatis (rulers of quadrants) for the different Ascendants as follows :

1. For Aries, Venus as the 7th lord and the waxing Moon as the 4th lord.
2. For Taurus, no planet comes under Kendradhipati Dosha.
3. For Gemini, Jupiter as the 7th and the 10th lord.
4. For Cancer, Venus as the 4th lord.
5. For Leo, Venus as the 10th lord.
6. For Virgo, Jupiter as the 4th and the 7th lord.
7. For Libra, the Moon, if strong, as the 10th lord.
8. For Scorpio, Venus as the 7th lord.
9. For Sagittarius, benefic Mercury as the 7th and the 10th lord.
10. For Capricorn, the Moon as the 7th lord, if waxing.
11. For Aquarius, no planet attracts Kendradhipati Dosha.
12. For Pisces, benefic Mercury as the 4th and the 7th lord.

For Taurus, Venus as the 1st lord is a natural benefic, so also for Libra. For Gemini and Virgo, Mercury, though the ruler of the 4th and the 10th respectively, being at the same time the Lagna lord, remains unaffected by Kendradhipati Dosha.

For Sagittarius and Pisces, Jupiter is the Ascendant lord and therefore, his lordship of the 4th and the 10th respectively, does not cause Kendradhipati Dosha.

For Capricorn and Aquarius, Venus, no doubt is the ruler of the 10th and the 4th respectively, both Kendras, but as he owns, at the same time, the 5th and the 9th respectively, he becomes a benefic and is free of Kendradhipati Dosha.

That means, Taurus and Aquarius are insured against Kendradhipati Dosha.

The Moon has Kendradhipati Dosha in the case of Aries, Libra and Capricorn but, generally, is not capable of major malefic results.

Mercury is a Kendra lord with its attendant evil, only if unafflicted by malefics Mars, Saturn, Sun, Rahu or Ketu for Sagittarius and Pisces.

Venus becomes an evil Kendra lord for both Cancer and Leo, ruling the 4th and the 10th respectively. For Aries and Scorpio, as 7th lord he assumes power to do evil.

Jupiter is malefic as the lord of a quadrant for Gemini and Virgo.

Coming to the degree of maleficence the Kendra lords are capable of, the normally best benefic Jupiter becomes the most malefic followed by Venus, then Mercury and lastly, the Moon for causing bad results in that order.

Therefore, the greatest impact of Kendradhipati Dosha falls on Gemini and Virgo natives. For both these Ascendants, Jupiter qualifies for Badhakahood also while as 7th lord, he can be a strong Maraka. However, he can be a partial Badhaka or a full-fledged one depending upon if Mandi is in Pisces or Sagitttarius. The condition of being the lord of the 22nd Drekanna and therefore acquiring Badhakattwa cannot be fulfilled by Jupiter for any of the three Drekannas rising in the Ascendants Gemini or Virgo. Therefore, if Jupiter is a full-fledged Badhaka by reason of Mandi being in a Jupiterean sign, this will tend to have the effect of aggravating the evil results Jupiter can give as Kendradhipati. Therefore, this combination of Marakattwa, Badhakattwa and Kendra lordship works to produce the greatest havoc in the lives of Gemini and Virgo natives where either the natural significations or the significations of the houses ruled by Jupiter are concerned. But Jupiter for such natives, if placed in the Upachayas (the 3rd, 6th, 10th or the 11th) or the trines (the 5th and the 9th), ceases to be an evil lord or effective malefic and may even promote the Bhavas he influences.

Chart 4: Born 20-2-1949 at 3-26 p.m. (IST) at 15 N 52, 74 E 32 with a balance of 3 years 0 months 6 days of Saturn Dasa at birth.

	RAHU 7-04		LAGNA 26-54
SUN 9-45 MARS 15-09	Chart 4 Rasi		
MERC 14-24 VENUS 25-51			SAT. (R) 11-31
JUPT. 29-58	MOON 14-30	KETU 7-04	

		MERC	LAGNA RAHU
MARS	Navamsa		SAT
			VENUS
	SUN JUPT. KETU	MOON	

In Chart 4, Jupiter as the 7th lord is a powerful malefic rendered doubly potent by his occupation of the 7th house, a Marakastana, and being a Badhaka lord. The 7th house ruling marital life was devastated by Jupiter. The first marriage ended in a bitter divorce accompanied by all the trauma such situations generate. Then came a second marriage which proved to be worse than the first. Not only was the wife immature and foolish but also proved unfaithful to the native robbing the native of both marital and mental peace.

The fact Jupiter occupies the 7th focussed the evil results more on marital matters.

The Hamsa Yoga generated by Jupiter occupying his Moolatrikona sign is, inspite of benefics also flanking it, rendered ineffectual since the Lagna lord is in the 8th, the worst Dustana.

In the case of a regional political figure (Chart 5), the same Ascendant Gemini rises in the Ascendant with the Ascendant lord Mercury and the Sun in the 9th. Jupiter in the 7th has caused Hamsa Yoga which has led to a mass following and political clout. But the 7th house is an empty void with marriage having eluded the native while personal life was marked by bitterness and frustration. Of course, the

Chart 5 : Born 24-2-1948 at 2-34 p.m. (IST) at 13 N 05, 80 E 18 with a balance of 2 years 8 months 23 days of Ketu Dasa at birth.

VENUS	RAHU		LAGNA	LAGNA	KETU MARS JUPT.	MOON
SUN MERC. (R)	Chart 5 Rasi		SAT. (R)	SAT. (R)	Navamsa	
			MOON MARS (R)	VENUS SUN		MERC. (R)
JUPT.		KETU			RAHU MERC.	

position of the Lagna lord and other Raja Yogas in the chart render it very strong. But Jupiter in the 7th has not helped 7th house matters and has worked only as Kendradhipati.

In two other cases of Gemini Ascendant, the 7th lord Jupiter in Libra (the 5th house) and Aries (the 11th house) respectively gave them understanding, affectionate and faithful spouses. Jupiter in the 9th too can cease to be harmful. But Jupiter even if a Kendra lord, in the 10th, an Upachaya, does not harm the native.

The position of the 7th and the 10th lord Kendradhipati Jupiter in the 10th from the Ascendant has taken away the sting of Kendradhipati Dosha in Chart 6.

The other sign of the Zodiac which has Jupiter coming under Kendradhipati Dosha is Virgo for which he becomes the 4th and the 7th lord. In both these houses, he wrecks havoc on domestic peace and marital life. In the 7th, Jupiter acquires multiple properties of Marakattwa, Badhakattwa and Kendradhipati Dosha generating much unhappiness in marital life. Otherwise, he may, as sometimes in the case of

Chart 6 : Born 2-6-1963 at 6-59 a.m. at 13 N 05, 80 E 18 with a balance of 1 year 11 months 23 days of Mars Dasa at birth.

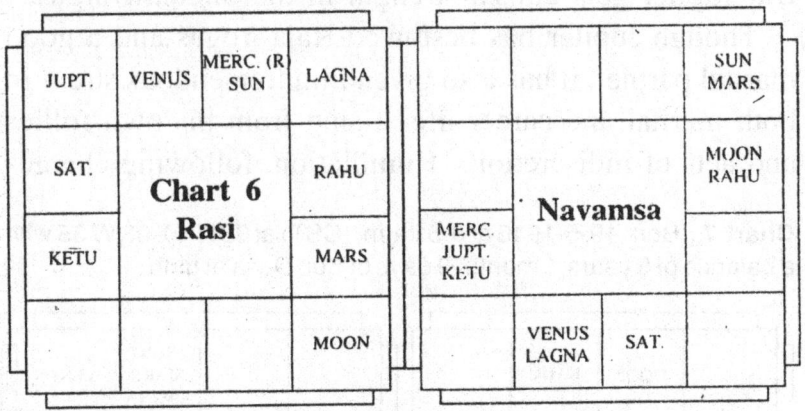

Gemini, deny one marital life. Or, if one gets married, Jupiter in the 7th will be out to wreak vengeance on the native. A Virgo native with Jupiter in the 7th married a beautiful girl who was both affectionate and accomplished. Marital life was exceedingly happy, in fact too good to be true. But Jupiter's power for evil did not leave them alone for long. Just months after the marriage, the native returned home from office to find his wife brutally murdered lying in a pool of blood. He has never quite recovered from shock.

In another case with Jupiter in the 4th for Virgo rising, the native had to undergo untold suffering, privation and humiliation in her marital home. The 4th house position of Jupiter causes a Hamsa Yoga, but thanks to an afflicted Ascendant and the Ascendant lord in a Dustana, the Yoga did not really materialize. Jupiter as Badhaka, Maraka and as Kendradhipati brought to bear his evil impact on domestic life.

The American President Clinton's is a clear example (Chart 7) of Jupiter's Kendradhipati Dosha working in a different manner. As 7th lord, he is a Kendra lord indeed. Further, he occupies the 2nd, a Maraka house. But Jupiter gets unusal strength in the Shodasavargas.

Though Jupiter has bestowed Raja Yogas and a good marital partner, it has also given him tremendous stress in both marital and career life arising from his own follies and acts of indiscretion. Humiliation, following charges

Chart 7 : Born 19-5-1946 at 8-51 a.m. (CST) at 33 N 40, 93 W 35 with a balance of 5 years 1 month 9 days of Sun Dasa at birth.

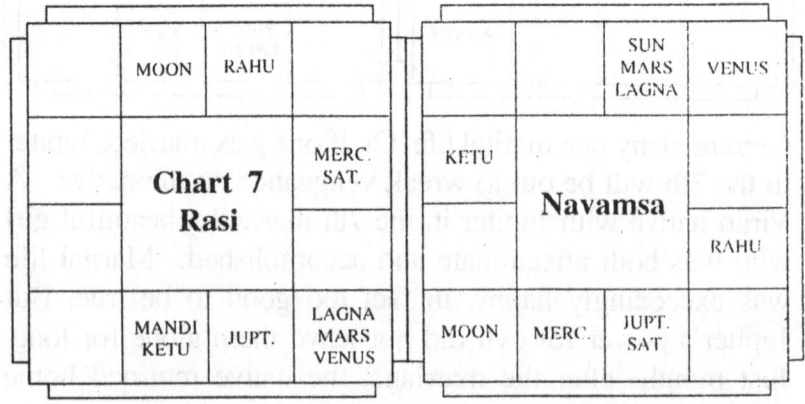

of impeachment, and marital estrangement have made Clinton's Presidency one of the most stormy and turbulent in the history of the country. Jupiter as Kendradhipati being in the 2nd house has also led to financial disaster for the man arising from the astronomical sums his law suits have cost him both in terms of legal fees and the compensation sums he has been asked to pay by the courts.

Jupiter in the 3rd, the 6th, the 10th and the 11th has not proved baneful to Virgo natives inspite of his Kendradhipati Dosha. In trines also, his power for evil has been transmuted into beneficence.

In a Dustana such as the 6th, the 8th and the 12th, Jupiter shows his power for evil, although the 6th being an Upachaya as well, the degree or intensity of evil gets vastly reduced.

Summing up, but only as far as Jupiter's Kendradhipati Dosha goes, both for Gemini and Virgo, his occupation of the 7th has a shattering influence on marital life. If in the 2nd (a Maraka house), it can damage finances, family, marital peace and career too. In the 3rd, Jupiter ceases to hurt. In the 4th again, Jupiter is upto mischief for both signs destroying domestic peace and hurting vocational life. In the 5th, he is welcome and benevolent. In the 6th, he even promotes career trinally aspecting the 10th but can be baneful for marriage. In the 8th, as 7th and 10th lord, for Gemini, in a Dustana, he attracts malefic results such as humiliation and false charges in career and physical and even emotional distancing from the spouse. For Virgo, Jupiter, in this Dustana as the 4th and the 7th lord while not harming the 4th too much can affect marital life and its durability adversely. In the 9th, Jupiter becomes generous and helpful conferring a good spouse and marriage. In the 10th, for Gemini, in his own sign Pisces, he is a powerfully helpful influence on career matters. For Virgo too, he gives stability and respect in one's vocational life. Marriage, in the both these cases, will be good. In the 11th again his power for evil is neutralised. In the 12th, the Kendradhipati Dosha has an adverse influence on marital life and happiness.

For Sagittarius and Pisces, it is Mercury as the 7th and 10th lord and as the 4th and the 7th lord respectively who gets Kendradhipati Dosha. Jupiter as the Ascendant lord becomes a first rate benefic. In the case of a Pisces native, Mercury as the 7th lord, though in his sign of exaltation in Virgo, deprived the native of the major significations of both houses coming under his rulership. The mother (4th house) was a mental patient and the native never got married (7th house). The same applies to Sagittarius natives. If Mercury, being the 7th and 10th lord, occupies the 2nd, the 4th, the 7th, the 8th or the 12th houses and if he is affliction-free, he creates a lacuna in the houses he is associated with.

A Sagittarius native with Mercury and the Sun in the 12th aspected by exalted Jupiter, inspite of excellent looks, education and family background, remains unmarried in her late forties. Countless proposals fizzled out for one reason or the other while her lesser peers are all married. The trinal postion between the Ascendant and the 7th lord Mercury should have actually helped but did not because of Mercury gaining three-fold nagative strength — Kendradhipati Dosha, Marakattwa and Badhakattwa — for evil. The fact Mercury is well-associated only worked against the native. The association of Mercury with the Sun is not an affliction.

The Moon as 4th lord for Aries, as 10th lord for Libra and as the 7th lord for Capricorn acquires Kendradhipati Dosha. But the Moon, to qualify for this Dosha, should be waxing and strong. Otherwise, he escapes the evil of Kendradhipati Dosha. But, as a general rule, the Moon's power to do evil is minimal and therefore, the Kendradhipati Dosha too, in effect, cannot be heavy. The Dasa of such a Moon may bring in setbacks in domestic life and health of mother, career and marital life respectively for Aries, Libra and Capricorn. It can also affect mental equipoise leading to severe depression or other states of mental aberration based on the planets influencing the Moon.

Moving on to Kendradhipati Dosha for Venus, Cancer Ascendant which becomes vulnerable to the affliction has Venus as 4th lord ruling happiness, mother, relatives, family property and vehicles. Venus generates problems in all these sectors of life. As Sukastanadhipati, the most afflicted in such cases is the family environment due to problems related to parents, siblings, relatives, children and spouse. Sometimes the foucs of the problem may be on one or more of these significations but predominantly it will involve the marital partner. In fact, it would almost seem like Kendradhipati Dosha is at the roof of the theory that Cancer Ascendants are usually unlucky or unhappy in their marriages. Venus as the 4th lord is also the Kalatrakaraka as well as Badhaka lord (being the 11th lord for the morveable sign) and therefore, brings in an element of tornment in married life, the degree of suffering dependent on other factors related to the 7th house. If Venus as Kalatrakaraka, under Kendradhipati Dosha, affects adversely marital happiness, can the same line of reasoning be extended to explore the possibility of Kendradhipati Jupiter having an adverse impact on his Karakattwa or natural signifactions, primarily progeny or children ? If Jupiter is in the 4th in Sagittarius or in the 7th in Pisces or in the 2nd, the 6th, the 8th or the 12th, then progeny can indeed be adversely affected. It can deny one issue or give sickly children or other adverse results related to children, the degree of adversity depending on other afflictions to the 5th house.

Returning to Venus, a classic example of the Kendradhipati Dosha of this planet is Nehru's case. His wife was sickly and died early. As Kendradhipati, Venus in the 4th, deprived the native of a marital life.

In the 11th house for Cancer Ascendant, Venus, though in his own house, can still affect the Karakattwa.

The native (Chart 8), coming from an orthodox South Indian Brahmin family, is involved with an American girl

Chart 8 : Born 11-4-1967 at 1-35 p.m. at 13N04, 80E 17 with a balance of 18 years 11 months 3 days of Venus Dasa at birth.

SUN 28-49 SAT. 12-44 MERC. 3-22	RAHU 16-03 MOON 14-03	VENUS 4-25		SUN			
	Chart 8 Rasi		JUPT. 3-11 LAGNA 20-04	KETU VENUS MARS (RS) LAGNA	Navamsa		JUPT. MOON
							RAHU MERC.
		MARS (R) 14-22 KETU 16-03				SAT.	

who already has a child by an earlier relationship. Marriage appears difficult because he will not marry without his parent's consent. And the poor parents cannot reconcile themselves to welcoming a daughter-in-law from a different race with a child that is not thier son's.

For Leo natives, Venus is the 3rd and 10th lord and therefore acquires Kendradhipati Dosha. The 10th house becomes vulnerable and the most times, the Dosha shows up in career matters or one's reputation falling under a shadow. The Karakattwa of Venus is relatively safe for Leo Ascendant unlike in the case of Cancer Ascendant where the 4th house and the Badhakattwa being both jointly involved, it is the Kalatra Bhava that takes the blow. Venus, if he occupies the 2nd, the 4th, the 7th or the 8th, can generate difficulties associated with the Bhavas or Karakattwa involved for these two Ascendants. But in the 3rd, the 5th, the 9th or the 11th and even the 12th, he becomes shorn of his power for evil.

For Aries and Scorpio, Venus is the lord of the 7th Kendra and this house covers marital life.

Chart 9 : Born 1-7-1961 at 7-45 p.m. (BST) at 52 N 50, 00 E 30 with a balance of 1 year 10 months 8 days of Mars Dasa at birth.

		VENUS	MERC. (R)	SUN	JUPT.		MARS RAHU
MOON KETU	Chart 9 Rasi			SAT. LAGNA	Navamsa		
JUPT. (R) SAT. (R)			MARS RAHU	MERC. VENUS			
	LAGNA			KETU		MOON	

Chart 9 is of Princess Diana who had the 7th lord Venus in the 7th in his own sign Taurus. This causes a Malavya Yoga that gave her the comfort and luxury that are the privilege of only royals. But as Kendradhipati in the 7th combined with Maraka powers, Venus shattered her marital life beyond repair.

Likewise for Aries Ascendants, Venus in the 7th in Libra, though in his Moolatrikona and capable of conferring other Venusian benefits, can mar marital happiness. In the 2nd also, Venus combines double Maraka powers and Kendradhipati Dosha for Aries Ascendants and becomes baneful. But for Scorpio, Venus in the 2nd is not as bad as for Aries for then, he will not have the Maraka lordship of the 2nd also as in the case of the latter.

Venus in the 4th for Aries or Scorpio rising is not a good thing to have and generates a void in this area. In a case of Aries rising with Venus in the 4th, the advent of his Dasa led to loss of spouse and a life of dependence on unloving relatives.

Venus in the Upachayas (the 3rd, the 6th, the 10th and the 11th) for Aries and Scorpio is not particularly harmful, although in the case of the 6th house (being the 12th from the 7th), he may regain his power to hurt. In the 2nd, the 4th, the 7th and the 8th, Venus becomes difficult. In the 1st, the 5th and the 9th, the Kendradhipati Dosha is greatly diluted or even diffused. Venus in the 12th also escapes the evil of Kendradhipati Dosha and in some cases, becomes positively good.

In Chart 10, Venus as the 7th lord is in the 12th.

Marital life has been good and even during Venus Dasa. it did not meet with any adverse situations.

If a planet acquires Kendradhipati Dosha in the Rasi chart, its malefic influence will undoubtedly show up irrespective of its position in the Varga charts. Its strength in the Varga charts is not an antidote for the evil of Kendradhipati Dosha. The Navamsa chart can be taken as a mild influence on the Rasi but only in a secondary sense. Therefore, whatever the Varga strength of a planet, it cannot supercede the Kendradhipati Dosha which has its origins in the Rasi chart. Even if Jupiter as 7th lord, has Shadvargabala, his Kendradhipati Dosha is not

Chart 10 : Born 14-11-1937 at 7-30 a.m. at 10 N 49, 79 E 50 with a balance of 1 year 5 months 10 days of Jupiter Dasa at birth.

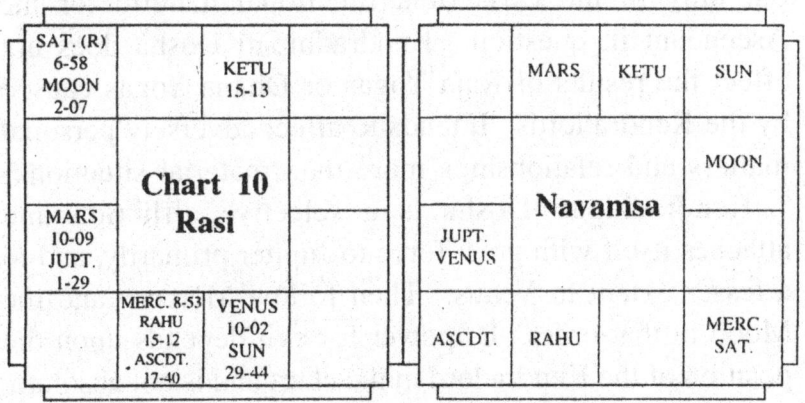

removed. It affects the marital relationship and domestic peace very badly. So also Venus and benefic Mercury, if Kendra lords.

Jupiter has the greatest Kendradhipati Dosha because this Dosha is aided by his Badhakattwa (full or partial) and Marakattwa. Venus comes next because Venus acquires Marakattwa in addition in the case of Aries and Scorpio and in the case of Cancer, though not affected by Marakattwa, there is Badhakattwa. For Leo Ascendants, Kendradhipati Dosha due to Venus is not affected by Badhakattwa or Marakattwa and so, may not be impactful as for Cancer Ascendant.

Kendradhipati Dosha is an affliction that hits only natural benefics and under certain conditions only, these conditions being dictated primarily by the houses occupied by the planets. The Dosha ceases to be effective when the Kendra lord associates with a trine (the 5th, 9th and 1st) or an Upachaya (the 3rd, 6th, 10th and 11th). Secondly, the Dosha surfaces in the strongest sense of the term during the Dasa of the Kendra lord. It can show up to a lesser degree in the Bhukti also of the Kendra lord but only in the Dasa of a functional malefic for the Ascendant in question. Kendradhipati Dosha does not affect the results of Raja Yogas or Dhana Yogas caused by the Kendra lords. It tends to affect adversely personal matters and relationships more than material situations.

Kendradhipati Dosha is a selective affliction and attaches itself with great force to Jupiter primarily, and to a lesser extent to Venus. Then follow Mercury and the Moon in that order. Its power for evil depends upon the position of the Kendra lord in the chart and is not absolute.

(09-11-'99)

Chapter 3

A Critical Examination of Dustanas

BRIHAT PARASARA HORA defines clearly the Dustanas in Chapter 7, Sloka 35 when it says, षष्टाष्टव्ययभावस्तु दु:संज्ञास्त्रिकसंज्ञका: । meaning, the 6th, the 8th and the 12th are Dustanas or Trikas. The definition says nothing about the results of these Bhavas but the use of the prefix *dus* (दुस्) carries clearly a negative implication indicative of the adverse role these Bhavas play in a chart.

Sloka 37 moves on to a brief and very quick classification of the 12 houses and their significations.

तनुर्धनं च सहजो बन्धुपुत्रारयस्तथा ।
युवतीरन्ध्रधर्मारव्य कर्मलाभव्यया: क्रमात् ॥

meaning, the body, wealth, co-borns, progeny, enemy, spouse (wife), adversity, Dharma and vocation, gain and loss respectively are the significations of the 12 Bhavas starting with the Ascendant.

According to this Sloka, the 6th, 8th and 12th houses govern negative areas of life while the remaining Bhavas rule the non-negative features of life.

In astrology, as in medicine, both subjects dealing with the conglomerate of body and mind, but astrology doing it at a more comprehensive, deeper and subtler level, there can be no strict compartmentalization into absolutely good or bad areas. A certain degree of overlapping becomes inevitable. In astrology, as the subject matter of its study is the highly complex intricacy called life, the diffusion between the good and bad segments is greater and naturally that much more complex. Nevertheless, there is a preponderance of malefic significations where the Dustanas are concerned. The Dustanas are not always evil, they can produce some highly desirable results too but their main theme certainly does not revolve around the palatable in life. They concern the adversities of life. It is from this angle, we shall try to make a humble effort to understand this much talked about but highly confusing concept of Dustanas.

The 6th house though called a Dustana is also one of the Upachayas (houses of elevation), the others being the 3rd, the 10th and the 11th. As an Upachaya, the 6th derives the property of giving beneficial results also but its Dustana results are not, therefore, disallowed from showing up.

For Taurus and Scorpio, the Ascendant lords Venus and Mars respectively, are also rulers of the 6th, a Dustana, but they are more benefic than malefic, the Ascendant lordship holding sway.

The 8th house is deemed to be malefic because it rules the 12th from the 9th which, as ruling fortune or Bhagya, is associated with favorable results (भाग्यव्ययाधिपत्येन रन्ध्रशो न शुभप्रद:). The Dustana tag to the 8th lord gets greatly loosened if he is, at the same time, the ruler of the Ascendant also according to **Jataka Chandrika** (I-8) : स एव शुभसन्घाता लग्नाधीशोsपि चेत्स्वयम् । This becomes possible in the case of Aries when Mars becomes a benefic, superceding the evil of his 8th house lordship and also in the case of Libra rising when its ruler Venus shares the

8th house lordship of Taurus with the Ascendant. the taint of the 8th lordship is not rigid for Aries and Libra Ascendants.

In Chart 11 of a Nobel Laureate, the Ascendant Aries rises with its ruler in the 8th house. The results of the Ascendant lord being relegated to the 8th house such as difficulties, penury or humiliation did not materialize. On the other hand, the Ascendant lord in the 8th not only

Chart 11 : Born 3-11-1933 at 3-40 p.m. (LMT) at 22 N 35, 88 E 21 with a balance of 1 year 8 months 5 days of Sun Dasa at birth.

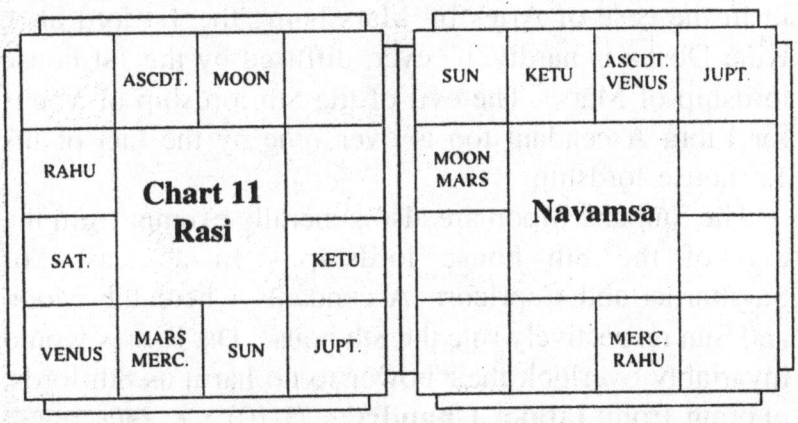

gave a solid foundation to the chart as a whole but was instrumental in taking the native to the pinnacle of academic success and recognition. But there are two angles to the positioning of Mars in the 8th house. As Ascendant lord, Mars in the 8th in his own sign, strengthens the Ascendant, and therefore, the chart as a whole and in turn, its potential for good results. But Mars considered as the generator of Kuja Dosha does not let go off his power for evil. The first marriage broke up bringing to the fore that as far as the evil of Kuja Dosha is concerned, even the fact of Kuja or Mars being the

Lagna lord may not always help. Nor has Mars strengthened the 8th house signification of *Mangalya* (marital bond) as 8th lord in the 8th. All other properties of Mars, whether as Lagna lord or as 8th lord, occupying his own sign became ineffective and only his power to cause harm to the marriage was left unfettered to wreak havoc in this specific area. But as far as the Dustana angle goes, the adverse influence was neutralised, even rendered favorable by Mars being the 8th lord. Therefore, we can conclude while the Dustana lordship can be reined in in the case of Aries by Mars being the 1st lord also. Kuja Dosha is hardly, if ever, diffused by the 1st house lordship of Mars. The evil of the 8th lordship of Venus for Libra Ascendant too is overcome by the fact of his 1st house lordship.

The Sun and Moon are also generally exempt from the evil of the 8th house lordship. In all cases of Sagittarius and Capricorn Ascendants where the Moon and Sun respectively rule the 8th house, Dr. RAMAN would invariably overlook their power to do harm as 8th lords, quoting from **Jataka Chandrika** (I-10) : न रन्ध्रेशत्वदोषस्तु सूर्याचन्द्रमसोर्भवेत् । That leaves us only with Jupiter (for Taurus and Leo Ascendants), Saturn (for Gemini and Cancer Ascendants) and Mercury (for Scorpio and Aquarius Ascendants) as evil 8th lords. Not to be overlooked in this classification are, however, Mars and Venus respectively as evil 8th lords but only for Virgo and Pisces Ascendants.

The last of the Dustanas and possibly, the least evil, is the 12th house. It derives its power to cause harm from the fact it is the व्ययस्थान (Vyayastana) or the house of loss from the Ascendant, the central pillar of a chart.

The Dosha of the 12th house lordship attaching to the 1st lord obtains only in the case of Saturn for Aquarius Ascendant. But even here, the lordship of the 1st house overpowers Saturn's lordship of the Dustana.

The Dustanas and their power to harm in increasing order of the 12th, 6th and 8th in terms of their significations, almost seems to echo the proverb "When money is lost, nothing is lost. When health is lost, something is lost. And when character is lost, everything is lost". Very broadly understood, the 12th rules financial losses, the 6th rules Roga or disease (loss of health) and the 8th, Parabhava or humiliation.

According to **Jataka Parijata** (XIII-71), the 6th Bhava is said to rule रोगारिव्यसनक्षतानि वसुधापुत्रारिश्चिन्तयेत् or diseases, enemies and bad habits as also wounds, Mars being the Karaka for these significations.

मरणहरणदासक्लेशविघ्नानि रन्ध्रात् or death, stealing, servant, suffering and obstacles are to be read from the 8th house.

Under the 12th house come expenditure, destruction, loss and downfall.

The Dustanas, in brief, are associated with adverse results generally. Malefics in the 6th, 8th or 12th from the Ascendant weaken the chart and show a preponderance of suffering to the native. A Capricorn native with the Sun and Saturn in the 8th leads a life of privation and hardship. Her own as well as her husband's educational qualifications and abilities do not appear to promise much in the future also.

When a Bhava lord occupies a Dustana from the Ascendant, then the Bhava concerned comes under baneful influences.

If the Ascendant lord is in the 12th, the 6th or the 8th from the Ascendant, one's health will not be satisfactory or one may have a difficult life.

If the 2nd lord be in a Dustana, the native will have much suffering, family problems and financial worries.

The 3rd lord in the 6th, 8th or the 12th may deprive one of relatives, and generally create problems with neighbours.

If the 4th lord be in the 6th, the 8th or the 12th, one may have difficulty in acquiring one's own house. Or one's house may be lost through fire, litigation or other reasons. There may also be difficulty in acquiring and maintaining one's own vehicle. Or one's vehicle may get involved in litigation or accident.

The 5th lord in a Dustana denies one academic opportunities. Even if they are available, one may be hampered from making the best of them due to reasons of ill-health, financial problems or an inability to assimilate or cope with the syllabus. Such a disposition may also lead to inadequate communication skills and depending upon the intensity of affliction, one may be even dumb or suffer from stammering. Childlessness or loss of children or unsuccessful pregnancies can also result from such a disposition.

The 6th lord in the 6th, the 8th or the 12th is a favorable disposition but the adverse results cannot be ruled out *in toto*.

The 7th lord in the 6th may bring in arbitration into the marriage. In the 8th, it can lead to loss of spouse and in the 12th, affect marital life adversely.

If the 7th lord is in the 8th, then marriage comes under a discount. It can be loss of spouse or other calamities that could hit marriage. A Gemini native with Jupiter in the 8th was invovled in a murder case within months of his marriage. He was taken into custody, and of course, this had an adverse repercussion on both marital life (7th) and reputation (10th) ruled by the Dasa lord Jupiter.

The native of Chart 12, a silk merchant, got married in the last Bhukti of Jupiter Dasa with Jupiter as 7th lord being in the 8th with the 8th lord. The wife died soon after in a fire accident. The fire also caused extensive damage to his stocks leading to great loss. Jupiter is also

Chart 12 : Born 24-11-1961 at 8-30 p.m. at 9 N 31, 77 E 41 with a balance of 17 years 0 months 2 days of Rahu Dasa at birth.

			ASCDT. MOON		ASCDT.	JUPT. RAHU	VENUS	MERC.
KETU		Chart 12 Rasi			SAT.	Navamsa		
JUPT. SAT.			RAHU					
	SUN MARS	MERC. VENUS				MOON	MARS	SUN KETU

the 10th lord. Both the 7th and 10th house significations were greatly harmed by the 8th house occupation of Jupiter.

The lord of the 8th in the 6th or the 12th, though good in some respects, can curtail longevity. The 8th lord in the 8th, however, promotes longevity.

The 9th lord in a Dustana, more especially the 8th, works against the native's interests in several ways bringing in major setbacks and calamities in life.

The 10th lord in a Dustana is not always bad and can give good results too. But, if in the 8th, under affliction, it may bring in humiliation in one's vocational life.

The 11th lord in a Dustana affects financial luck, denies one older siblings or brings in problems on their account.

If the Dustana involved is the 12th, then the results of the Bhava concerned get harmed. The 4th or 9th lord, for instance, in the 12th may deprive one of mother or father respectively or create some kind of lacunae in these areas.

When a Bhava lord is in the 6th, the 8th or 12th from that Bhava, it weakens and harms the Bhava in question.

This is paritcularly so when judging Ayus or longevity. The 8th lord in the 7th (which is the 12th from the 8th) can often lead to early death. So also the 8th lord in the 12th from Lagna.

The 8th lord Saturn, *prima facie*, appears strong being in his own sign Capricorn and in the 7th where he gets Digbala in Chart 13. But considered from the 8th house Aquarius, Saturn is in the 12th from the 8th. The native died in her early twenties.

When the 7th lord is in the 6th (the 12th from the 7th) then marital life becomes vulnerable to upheavals. Marital life never really took off for a Scorpio native with Venus in Aries (the 12th from the 7th) when her husband was taken into custody on charges of murder a few weeks after the marriage.

Litigation, which can be broadly described as trouble from enemies or adversaries, can also be examined from a study of the 6th house.

A Critical Examination of Dustanas

Chart 13 : Born 19-10-1959 at 11-45 p.m. (IST) at 20 N 56, 77 E with a balance of 11 months 5 days of Sun Dasa at birth.

KETU 10-45	MOON 7-56			MOON	RAHU	MARS	
	Chart 13 Rasi		LAGNA		**Navamsa**		SAT.
SAT.			VENUS 19-36				LAGNA
	SUN 3-46 MARS 7-03 MERC 23-39	RAHU 10-45		MARS	SUN	JUPT. KETU	

Chart 14 has 6th lord Jupiter in the 7th aspecting the Ascendant strongly. His retrogression caused by debilitated Badhaka Sun only added to his maleficence. The Dasa of the 6th lord Jupiter began in 1991. Just before that,

Chart 14 : Born 11/12-11-1964 at 5-23 a.m., at 13 N, 77 E 35 with a balance of 1 year 0 months 21 days of Moon Dasa at birth.

	JUPT.(R)	RAHU		MANDI	KETU		SUN
SAT.	**Chart 14 Rasi**			ASCDT.	**Navamsa**		MOON MARS VENUS
MOON			MARS				
KETU	MERC	ASCDT. SUN	VENUS	JUPT	SAT.	MERC RAHU	

the native bought a lorry for business purposes. When he found he was not able to get profits by transporting goods in it, he sold it off for what he thought was a good price to a starlet. This was at the fag end of Rahu Dasa. He made two mistakes, one of which, especially would plague him through Jupiter Dasa with Jupiter being the malefic 6th lord. After receiving only a small sum as token payment for the sale and before the registration papers of the new owner were processed, he handed delivery of the lorry to the buyer. The lorry was still registered in the native's name when it met with a serious accident. The native is caught in litigation related to the accident. He has not received the full amount for the lorry from the buyer, either.

This case is also a good illustration for a little used principle (**Brihat Parasara Hora**. Chap.8, Sl. 39-43) which treats the Karaka as the Ascendant for analysing matters related to the Karakattwa, and to which the Dustana theory can also be applied. Here, Venus is the Karaka for vehicles. Jupiter is in the 8th from Venus. The 8th is the strongest of the malefic houses. Destruction and problems through the lorry have been the result in Jupiter Dasa. Additionally, we note that the 6th, 8th and 12th (all Dustanas) from the Karaka Venus are occupied by malefics adding to the affliction to the Karaka.

Malefics in the 6th, the 8th or 12th from any particular Bhava also are said to damage or even destroy that Bhava.

The Bhava for vehicles is the 4th house which is Capricorn in this case. There is Rahu in the 6th from it, Mars in the 8th and Ketu in the 12th from it. The damage to the 4th Bhava is obvious. But we must note if the 8th Bhava had been free of malefics, then Rahu and Ketu in the 6th and 12th respectively, could have promoted the

Bhava instead in accordance with the generally accepted rule of Rahu being favorable in the 6th.

The 4th house or Matrustana and the Moon as Matrukaraka also stand to suffer because of malefics in the Dustanas from both. The native's mother is a diabetic and has lost her vision. Other health problems have, more or less, made her an invalid. The native is the only one of three siblings who has taken on the responsibility of taking care of his mother with its attendant difficulties and tensions of day-to-day life.

The relegation of the Ascendant lord Venus to the 12th house has made the native vulnerable to a life of difficulties.

The 6th occupied or aspected by benefics guards one from enemies. So also a strong 6th lord.

Such a disposition protects one from the evil machinations of jealous relatives, rivals and others who may be inimically disposed towards the native. Jupiter in the 6th is said to help one overcome adversaries. The Sun

Chart 15 : Born 24-3-1963 at 8-55 p.m. at 13 N 00, 77 E 35 with a balance of 4 years 11 months 8 days of Jupiter Dasa at birth.

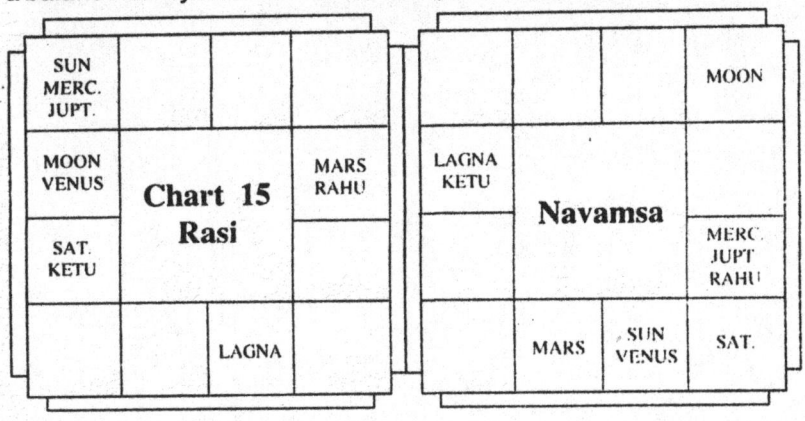

in the 6th in a friendly sign or in exaltation makes one respected and stand out amongst one's relatives and protects one from inimical forces.

The 6th house in Chart 15 is Pisces occupied by 6th lord Jupiter which renders it strong. The Sun also there is in strength. This has resulted in giving the native highly favorable results despite scheming by ill-disposed relatives and in-laws. The native was able to get married to a good-natured highly qualified husband even as her relatives tried to cancel and thwart the marriage. She was able to go overseas in the Dasa of Mercury who is in the 6th, and where she now leads an independent and happy life with her husband and child. (09-2000)

Chapter 4

Enemies from the Sixth House

4

DEPENDING UPON the planet in the 6th house and afflicting it, one may have to face continuing annoyance from the class of people represented either by the planet or its Karakattwa or the Bhava which it owns. If the Sun is in debility or in an unfriendly sign in the 6th, the native may prove inimical to his own father by teaming up with the latter's rivals or adversaries.

If the 6th house has a debilitated Jupiter or Jupiter afflicts it in other ways then one may face hostility or harassment from the University or teaching staff. As Jupiter is the Karaka for the 5th one may even antagonise members of the student community and invite problems.

Chart 16 : Born 21-6-1990 at 1-00 p.m. (ZST) at 44 N 26, 26 E 06 with a balance of 3 years 9 months 12 days of Moon Dasa at birth.

		VENUS (R)	SUN MANDI		RAHU	ASCDT	MOON
KETU			MERC	MANDI			MERC JUPT
	Chart 16 Rasi		MARS JUPT SAT RAHU		Navamsa		
			ASCDT MOON	SUN MARS SAT		KETU	VENUS

Or one may find oneself in a volatile situation involving students or eductional institutions.

The native of Chart 16 escaped alive unhurt in a shoot-out on 20-4-1999 at about mid-day in a small town school in the USA when two boys went wild shooting fatally 12 classmates and a teacher before they turned the guns on themselves. As the shooting began, the boys ran helter skelter and one of them caught in the melee was the native.

The 6th lord Saturn is in very close conjunction with 8th lord Mars and 7th lord Jupiter with Rahu also joining them in the 12th.

This is a very good example of the dictum that the *6th lord, occupant and planet aspecting it, if malefic and weak, cause, among other results, danger from enemies.* The 6th has Ketu aspected by afflicted 6th lord Saturn, afflicted 8th lord Mars and malefic 7th lord Jupiter who, in turn, is afflicted by Rahu, both being in the same Nakshatra Makha. Mars brought in violence while Jupiter led to danger from fellow-students in a school premises. Jupiter being the Karaka of both student (*sishya*) and teaching institution.

This chart is also a good example for the Yoga —

शत्रुस्थानाधिपे दुःस्थे नीचमूढारिराशिगे ।
लग्नेशे बलसंयुक्ते शत्रुनाशं वदेद्बुध ॥

meaning, *when the 6th lord is in a Dustana and depressed, combust or in inimical sign and lord of Lagna is possessed of strength, it shows destruction of (or total protection from) enemies.*

The 6th lord Saturn in Chart 16 is afflicted by his degree conjunction with Mars in the 12th in an inimical sign Leo and star Uttarashada attracting enemies and danger of violence through them. But the Lagna Virgo is quite powerful with not only its ruler Mercury in the 11th Vargottama but also in an exchange of signs with 11th lord Moon, which saved the native from any injury, and even death in the mad shooting which took a toll of many other innocent lives.

The term 'enemy' under the 6th house signification does not necessarily imply personal animosities although such relations cannot be ruled out *in toto*. What it points to is forces that could prove inimical to one's interest and well-being. It can show inflamed passions, again not specifically always directed at the native, as leading to dangerous situations in which such natives could get caught unwittingly also as in the case of violent riots and demonstrations.

If Mars is afflicted in the 6th joined by the Sun or Rahu, then one will be exposed to danger from robbers, anti-social elements, militants and terrorists and sometimes, even by members of the police or defence forces.

Venus, so afflicted or afflicting the 6th, makes for rivals from the show or art world, from womenfolk generally, female relatives or even one's own wife (or husband), becoming inimical to one's interests.

Mercury gives one constant problems from the business community — may be banking organisations, businessmen and even small time traders and pedlars like vegetable or fruit vendors. Or, one may get into complicated situations involving conmen.

The afflicted Moon exposes one to danger from mobs and the public.

The Moon, Mars and Rahu or Saturn in the 6th can make one get caught in riots, communal or group clashes.

dacoities, stampedes or public demonstrations and thereby suffer much bodily, financially and in other ways.

The Sun when so involved may push a native into a tangle of complications involving tax or other governmental and quasi-governmental authorities with endless running around to get out of the problems.

When Saturn is the afflicting influence on the 6th house, the source of one's problems can be members of the labour class, small time criminals, household staff, servants, factory wrokers and even those in the trade unions.

In all cases, where enemies are concerned. *if out of the 6th occupant, the 6th lord or the planet aspecting the 6th, at least two are exceedingly well-placed and strong, then they result in overcoming or terminating the adversary or adversity quickly. Even if one of these factors is strong, the trouble from the inimical factor (or ailment) will operate only for a short time.*

A Leo native with Mars and Rahu in the 6th house and 6th lord Saturn exalted was attacked by lethal weapons by trade unionists but luckily escaped unhurt with Mars and Saturn being in strength. But their 6th house connection did expose him to the plot hatched by violent factory workers.

If the 6th lord, the 6th occupant and the planet aspecting it are all malefic and weak, it leads to destruction of property, danger from adversaries and disease. But if all these factors are well-placed and strong favorable results come with good health and enemic being routed.

The 6th lord is in the 6th afflicted by Saturn and Ketu in Chart 17. The 6th occupants Venus, Mars and Saturn are afflicted by Ketu. The Moon (in the 12th) who aspects the 6th and its occupants is eclipsed by Rahu and is aspected by malefics Mars and Saturn. The affliction from the Nodal axis to the 6th house factors is to be particularly noted.

Chart 17: Born 5-1-1928 at 5-26 p.m. (IST) at 27 N 27, 68 E 08 with a balance of 3 years 9 months 27 days of Mars Dasa at birth.

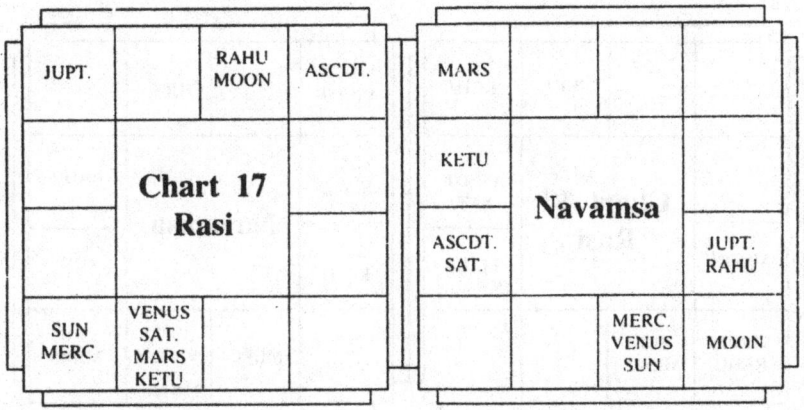

The native, prime minister of a neighbourng country, was arrested and put in jail by his political adversaries. After a year of humiliation and a complete breakdown of health due to neglect and squalid prison conditions, he was hanged to death.

Even if two out of the above 3 factors are well-placed in a Kendra, Trikona or the 11th in strength, then it helps to overcome the adverse indications of the 6th house quickly.

In Chart 18, the 6th lord Jupiter is Vargottama in the 11th and well-placed. The 6th occupant Venus gains from an exchange of signs with Vargottama Jupiter. The native who held the prime minister's office for nearly 16 years was an almost invincible force in the political life of the country. Even when she lost power temporarily, she was able to bounce back with renewed strength.

When the Ascendant lord is with a malefic in the 6th, the 8th or the 12th, bodily well-being (देहसौख्यं) will be lacking.

Chart 18 : Born 19-11-1917 at 11-13 p.m. (IST) at 25 N 27, 81 E 51 with a balance of 1 year 3 months 25 days of Sun Dasa at birth.

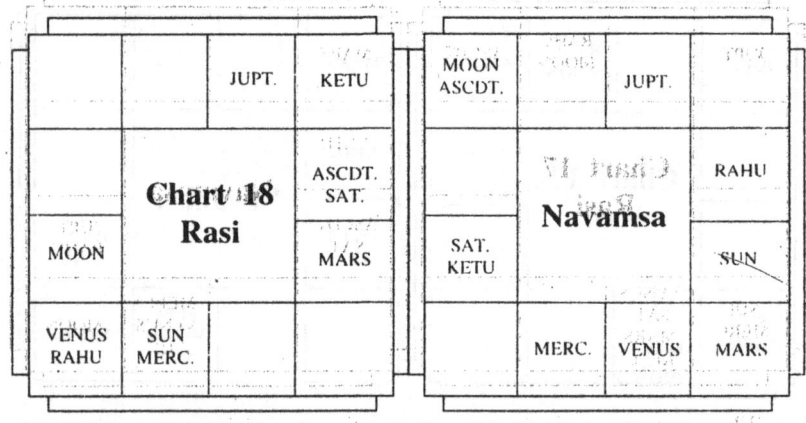

Such natives may suffer from poor health, weak constitution and low resistance. If other factors are also adverse, they become vulnerable to serious and chronic ailments. A Cancer Ascendant native with the Moon and Saturn in the 1st house was always going down with respiratory problems and wheezing.

Slightly better than the Ascendant lord himself being relegated to a Dustana is the sign-dispositer of the Ascendant lord (not being in a Dustana) being in a Dustana. But here also, physical health will generally be poor, the difference being in degree only. Constant aches and pains and mild infections and fevers will be a routine feature of their lives. Depending upon the nature of the sign involved, they may be emaciated and skinny also.

The 6th house is generally the best guide to understand the nature and duration of health problems one may come under.

Different planets in the 6th predispose the body to different kinds of aliments.

The Sun can show heart ailments, eye problems, dyspepsia, burning sensation in the stomach and gastritis.

The Moon can lead to weak digestion, nausea and loose motions.

Mercury shows convulsions, epileptic fits and nervous disorders.

Mars causes rashes, boils, skin eruptions, ulcers, acidity and a toxic state of blood.

Jupiter leads to rheumatic pains, diabetes, swellings, obesity.

Venus gives problems in the reproductive organs.

Saturn gives joint-related ailments, arthritis, bone-dislocations, spinal problems.

The 6th lord aspecting the Ascendant makes one weak and vulnerable to ailments. Even the association of the 6th lord with the Lagna lord is a distinct disadvantage for physical health. A Leo native with Saturn in the 7th is constantly plagued by severe digestive problems while a Sagittarian woman with Ascendant Jupiter joined by 6th lord Venus, though exceedingly attractive and comely in looks, is a diabetic and suffers poor health.

The Lagna lord with Mercury and 6th lord joined by Rahu, makes one incapable of normal marital life. If Mars joins the 6th and Ascendant lord combination, it leads to damage to the organ of generation by ulcers or other wounds. Venus joined by the 7th and 6th lords also leads to impotency with regard to one's wife. When malefics conjoin the 6th lord in the Ascendant, it afflicts the native with an ulcer or wound.

The 6th lord Moon in the Ascendant with the Sun and the 8th lord Mercury lead to cancer of the throat in Chart 19.

Chart 19 : Born 18-2-1836 at about 6-23 a.m. (LMT) at 22 N 53, 87 E 44 with a balance of 12 year 1 month 6 days of Jupiter Dasa at birth.

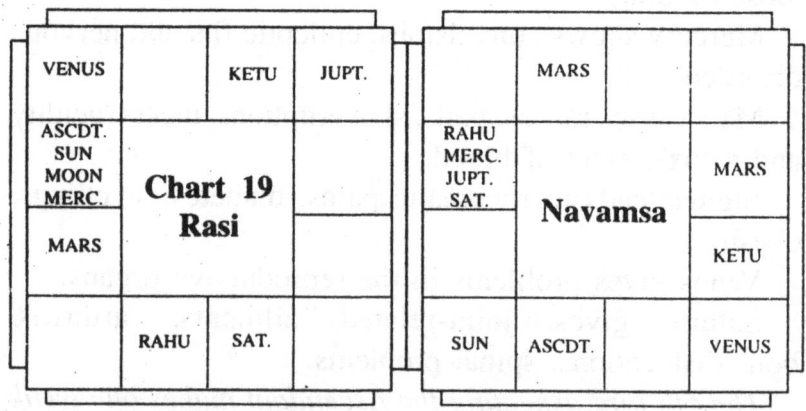

If the Lagna lord joins or is aspected by the 6th lord in the 8th, there is a problem in the anus.

The Lagna lord, Mars and Mercury together in the 6th or aspecting the 6th shows a nasty disease in the anus or piles.

If the Lagna lord is conjoined or aspected by Mercury from the 6th, it leads to an ulcer or wounds in the private parts.

The 6th lord between malefics is also not desirable.

When the Sun is joined by a malefic in the 6th, the disease will be due to excess of bile.

When Mars joins Mercury in the 6th in a malefic Navamsa aspected by the Moon and Venus, the disease will be due to a morbid state of phlegm.

The 6th lord joined by a malefic in the 1st shows ulcers in the body.

When the Lagna lord and the 6th lord combine with the Sun, fevers are a regular feature.

When the Lagna lord and 6th lord combine with the Moon, one becomes vulnerable to water accidents.

When the Lagna lord and 6th lord combine with Mars, one may face danger in war or through fire or heat boils.

When the Lagna lord and the 6th lord combine with Mercury, health problems are due to bile. When the Lagna lord and 6th lord combine with Jupiter, one is generally immune from disease.

When the Lagna lord and 6th lord combine with Saturn, windy complaints (*vayu*-related) like bodily aches, rheumatic disorders or arthritis are possible.

When the Lagna lord and 6th lord combine with Venus, one may be plagued by gynaecological problems.

The Moon and Mars in the 6th show jaundice and vomitting, while the Sun joining them can indicate colic.

The 6th house can also give clues to the health problems of others.

If a malefic joins the 6th lord and the 5th lord, one's father or son may be afflicted by an ulcer, wound or sore. If this combination involves the 4th house, the mother of the native will be the victim.

In Chart 20, the 6th lord Mars is joined by 4th lord Mercury and Rahu, all these planets being in the 4th.

Saturn also afflicts these planets by aspect. The mother of the native had cancer.

Chart 20 : Born 21/22-9-1957 at 0h.55m. (IST) at 13N, 77E35 with a balance of 4 years 4 month 12 days of Sun Dasa at birth.

KETU	MOON		ASCDT.	MERC.	ASCDT. RAHU		VENUS MARS SAT.
	Chart 20 Rasi				SUN	Navamsa	
			VENUS (R)	MOON			JUPT.
SAT.	JUPT.		SUN MERC. RAHU MARS			KETU	

If the planet so afflicted is the 7th lord, then it is the wife. If the 9th, one's maternal uncle. If the 3rd, one's younger brother will suffer from ulcer or wounds (व्रण). If the 11th, one's elder brother is similarly afflicted. But in all these cases, no conclusion should be made without a careful examination of the chart of the relative involved.

When the 6th lord is in a Dustana and depressed, in an inimical sign or combust but the lord of Lagna is strong, then it shields one from disease.

Likewise, when the 6th lord has attained Gopuramsa or other higher Vaiseshikamsas and is aspected by the Sun and the lord of Lagna is in full strength, it becomes good for the chart. (*12-2000*)

Chapter 5

The Eighth House and Calamities

Chapter 5

The Eighth Mother
and Catechumen.

5

THE 8TH HOUSE, the worst of the three Dustanas, draws its power to harm from it rulership of the 12th (decimation) from the 9th which rules Bhagya or fortune. The 8th house strikes at the very roots of the Bhagyastana with destructive effect.

The 8th also assumes importance as it rules longevity or the duration of life. The 8th lord, the 8th occupant, the planet aspecting the 8th, the ruler of the 22nd Drekanna, the planet joining the 8th lord from the Ascendant and the lord of the 64th Navamsa occupied by the Moon are called Chidragrahas and show vulnerable or calamitous points in life. Besides, it is the 8th house that brings in rude jolts in life that can throw everything out of gear.

The 8th house in certain combinations with other planets produces Yogas that deprive one of education and wealth, make one exceedingly wrathful, disagreeable in nature, cunning, shameless, filled with jealousy and rage and devoid of self-respect. It gives an extremely arrogant nature as well. It can make one an atheist also. One may be ugly or even deformed and take to begging. Depending on the intensity of the afflictions, all or some of these results may show up.

These results occur when :

(1) The Lagna lord has no strength and is aspected by the 8th lord while Jupiter is combust.

(2) When the 8th and 9th lords are in the 5th, the Lagna lord is in debility and the 4th lord is aspected by the 6th lord.

(3) When benefics are in the 8th, 6th and 12th and malefics are in the Kendras and Trikonas with the 11th lord being weak.

(4) When the Lagna lord is in the 8th, the 6th or the 12th without strength and 3 planets are in debility or combust.

(5) When Jupiter as 8th or 1st lord is stronger than the 9th lord with the 11th lord not being in a Kendra and is conjunct the Sun and weak.

(6) When Jupiter, Mars, Saturn or Mercury in debility is combust in the 6th, 8th or 12th.

(7) When Jupiter is in debility in the 6th, 8th or 12th.

These combinations, if present in a chart, especially in the period of the planets in the Dustanas, bring in huge losses and difficulties that can sometimes wipe out one's career and life.

Chart 21 : Born 25-3-1959 at 7-30 p.m. (IST) at 15 N 11, 76 E with a balance of 0 years 5 months 21 days of Moon Dasa at birth.

SUN MERC. (R) KETU	VENUS	MARS	
	Chart 21 Rasi		
SAT.			MOON RAHU ASCDT.

			MANDI RAHU
	Navamsa		
		KETU	VENUS SAT.
		MERC.	MARS ASCDT.

Benefic Venus is in a Dustana in Chart 21. Jupiter is not in a Kendra or trine. Malefics Saturn, Sun, afflicted Mercury and Rahu are in Kendras. The 8th and 9th lords are in an adverse exchange of signs. The 11th lord Moon, though Full, is heavily afflicted in the Ascendant. The 6th lord Saturn is adversely aspected by 8th lord Mars. The native who was in the business of garment exports suffered heavy losses running into crores. His factory had to close down and he is caught in several court cases. Combinations 2 and 3 can be modified and applied to this case. The 2nd lord Venus is in the worst Dustana showing the heavy financial liabilities of the native. The 8th lord Mars in the 9th has damaged the 9th house rendered worse by its ruler Venus being in a Dustana (12th) from the 9th.

Chart 22 : Born 7-5-1969 at 5-58 a.m. at 13 N 01, 76 E 03 with a balance of 4 years 4 months 9 days of Sun Dasa at birth.

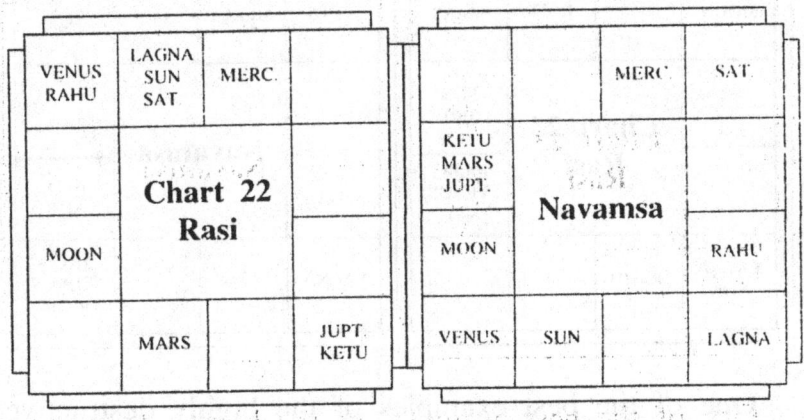

Chart 22 is another study in how Dustanas work. The 2nd lord Venus is in the 12th and the 6th lord Mercury is in the 2nd showing heavy financial liabilities following closure of a business unit. Combination (3) can be applied to this case. Benefics are in Dustanas (the 6th and the 12th) while the malefics are in Kendras. The 11th lord Saturn in Lagna in his sign of debility is with inimical Sun.

The 6th lord Mercury is in the 2nd showing financial problems. The 9th lord is afflicted in the 6th, a Dustana, and so also Lagna lord Mars in the 8th aspected by the 6th lord Mercury. The last factor is, however, the saving grace also of the chart. The Ascendant lord Mars though in the 8th is not tainted thereby. He shows a good inheritance protecting the native in contrast to Chart 21 where the Ascendant lord is heavily afflicted, and therefore, has weakened the base of the chart.

Chart 23 : Born 18-7-1919 at 6-17 p.m. at 12 N, 76 E 38 with a balance of 11 years 6 months 22 days of Saturn Dasa at birth.

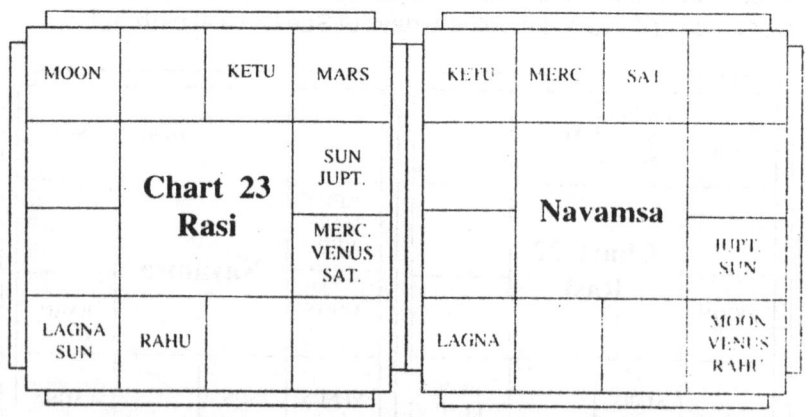

One of the best examples of the highly destructive nature of the 8th house is to be found in the case of the Maharajah of Mysore, the late Sri Jaya Chamarajendra Wodeyar (Chart 23). A scholar and a man of exemplary conduct, the Maharajah was humiliated by the country when the privy purse and other privileges promised to him on the eve of Indian Independence were summarily and arbitrarily withdrawn by the Government of India.

The Ascendant is the powerful sign Sagittarius which rises in Vargottama strength. The Ascendant is aspected by the 12th lord Mars. The Ascendant lord Jupiter is exalted in the 8th showing his royal birth and inheritance. He is with 9th lord Sun who thereby damages the chart in its entirety shifting the focus from the 9th to the 8th, from the best trine to the worst Dustana, thereby sowing the seeds of Yogabhanga in the chart. The Maharajah never quite recovered from the blow to his self-respect. The 10th lord Mercury is in the 12th from the 10th joined by malefic 6th lord Venus all adding up to loss of honour and of great wealth.

If there is a connection between the 8th and 10th houses, then one may suffer loss of job or reputation as

Chart 24 : Born 29-7-1954 at 10-32 a.m. (IST) at 18 N 58, 72 E 50 with a balance of 16 years 11 months 23 days of Saturn Dasa at birth.

Chart 24 Rasi				Navamsa			
			MERC. JUPT. RAHU		LAGNA JUPT. KETU	MERC.	
			SUN MANDI				
			VENUS	SAT.			MOON
MARS RAHU		SAT.	LAGNA	SUN	VENUS	RAHU	

the 10th is connected with vocation, honour and public image. Such a disposition also covers cases of summary termination of service or suspension. A Leo native with Venus in the 8th was arbitrarily dispensed with by the company he was working for under a contract. While the pain of humiliation could not be avoided, the 8th house showing inheritance and windfalls helped him get a tidy sum in settlement.

The native of Chart 24 was involved in a nation-rocking scandal related to stocks and shares. He was arrested and several cases were filed against him. The 8th lord

Chart 25 : Born 28-6-1921 at 1-00 p.m. (IST) at 18 N 00, 79 E 25 with a balance of 6 years 7 months 25 days of Saturn Dasa at birth.

MOON	KETU VENUS		SUN MARS MERC.		KETU		MERC.
	Chart 25 Rasi		JUPT. SAT.	SUN MARS	Navamsa		ASCDT
		RAHU	ASCDT	VENUS SAT.		MERC. JUPT. RAHU	

Mars is in the 4th aspecting the 10th house, 10th lord Mercury and 10th occupant Jupiter. The 2nd lord Venus is in the 12th, a Dustana, while the 6th lord Saturn is exalted in the 2nd. Saturn is also the 5th lord ruling speculation. The native is caught in mind-boggling litigation and problems related to stocks and shares. The chart is otherwise quite powerful; in fact, so strong that his word had greater credibility than a former prime minister's who was also caught in scams.

Chart 25 is a very interesting case of how the 8th and 10th house connection can bring humiliation and disgrace in one's life. The Ascendant lord Mercury Vargottama in the 10th house, the strongest of the Kendras, took the native to the highest office in the Central Government. But Mercury as 10th lord also is with 8th lord Mars and 12th lord Sun. The two malefics are in exact conjunction with Mars also being retrograde, aggravating his power for evil. In October 2000, the native was convicted in a bribery case with the sentence carrying a jail term also. Although there has been an appeal against it, the fact remains that the native has been the only prime minister of the country being convicted for such an offence.

(03-2001)

Chapter 6

Miscellaneous Matters
from Dustanas

THE 8TH HOUSE rules longevity and therefore death as well as its nature. In fact, the 8th and the 6th lords can be examined to time death. If a malefic is in the 6th or 8th from the Ascendant and if the 6th or the 8th itself is owned by a malefic, death may be said to take place in the Bhukti of the planet in the 6th or 8th in the Dasa of a planet conquered in planetary war.

Planets aspecting the 8th show the nature of death and the cause of death. If benefic influences are predominant, death is natural and due to health reasons or old age.

Chart 26 : Born 17-9-1906 at 7-23 a.m. (IST) at Colombo with a balance of 19 years 5 months 3 days of Venus Dasa at birth.

			JUPT.
SAT.	**Chart 26** **Rasi**		RAHU
KETU			MARS MERC. MOON
		VENUS	ASCDT. SUN

	VENUS SAT. JUPT.		KETU
	Navamsa		ASCDT. MARS
	SUN		MOON
	RAHU	MERC.	

- Chart 26 is one of the most interesting cases in recent history and is of a deceased President of Sri Lanka who crossed his 90th year and died a natural death. Even when he was targeted and a bomb hurled at him, it only killed the man sitting beside him, leaving the native untouched but only somewhat startled by the explosion so very close to him.

The 8th house Aries is aspected by only Venus and Saturn from his own sign. As Saturn occupies his Moolatrikona *cum* own sign as 6th lord and is in the Nakshatras of natural benefic Jupiter, he ceases to be harmful and only the benefic influence of Venus works on the 8th house showing death due to old age.

When the 6th house comes under malefic influences, death occurs due to accident, murder or suicide. In other words, malefic influences on the 8th point to unnatural causes of death. Such malefics are usually Mars, Saturn, Rahu, Ketu, waning Moon and afflicted Mercury. For example, if Lagna or Chandra Lagna is Aries and the 8th house is occupied or aspcted by Mars or Saturn or both, then a painful end is indicated. But, if Lagna or Chandra Lagna is Taurus, even if Jupiter is a powerful malefic, his influence on the 8th cannot, by itself, show a painful end. Only natural malefics bring about a difficult or violent death. But if the 8th house is aspected or occupied by a benefic, then the end is painless and natural. In the same case of Aries as Ascendant or Moon-sign, if Jupiter or Venus or both occupy Scorpio and no malefics influence them, the end will be peaceful and painless. Under such deaths can be classified deaths following sudden heart attacks, fevers, pneumonia and other causes which may give some mild discomfort before the body is shed. Painful deaths, on the other hand, may be deaths due to accident, suicide, attack and involving violence in some way or the other. Deaths that sometimes occur following or in the course of surgery also come under this category.

When the chart shows natural death and a strong planet aspects the 8th Bhava, inflammation or a disturbance in the humour ruled by that planet leads to death (तद्धातुकोपान्). If such a planet be the Sun, it will be an ailment caused by a burn (अग्नि) ; if the Moon, from a disease caused by water (जल); if Mars, from a disorder arising from a wound inflicted by a weapon (आयुध); if Mercury, from fever (ज्वर); if Jupiter, from a phlegm-related sickness (कफ); if Venus, hunger; and Saturn, from a disease arising from thirst.

1. When the waning Moon in the 8th is aspected strongly by Saturn, death may follow an agonising disease in the anus or through a Sastra (शस्त्र) or weapon.

2. When the Sun, Mars and Moon with Saturn are in the 8th, a strong storm in the mountains, thunderclap or lightning or a wall can lead to death.

3. If Mars and Sun are in exchange of signs and in a Kendra from the 8th lord, death occurs due to displeasure of sovereign and by impaling at the stake or other instrument of execution (शूलादिकायुध वरैर्निधनं समेति). This would cover all cases of death by execution — hangman's noose, electric chair and any other forms which the State follows in carrying out the judicial order of death sentence.

In Chart 27, we find the 8th house from Lagna aspected by Mars. From Chandra Lagna, there is Mars in the 8th. Both factors point to unnatural death. Additionally, the Sun and Mars have exchanged signs and if this Parivartana

Yoga is reckoned from Chandra Lagna, then the 3rd condition of both planets being in a Kendra from the 8th lord given above is also fulfilled. The results cannot be taken too literally. The native did not die due to the displeasure of the government but was assassinated by her own guards and shot dead.

Chart 27: Born 19-11-1917 at 11-13 p.m. (IST) at 22 N 27, 81 E 51 with a balance of 1 year 3 months 22 days of Sun Dasa at birth.

		JUPT. (R) 16-30	KETU 12-01
MOON 7-03	Chart 27 Rasi		ASCDT. 19-13 SAT. 22-1
			MARS 17-50
VENUS 22-28 RAHU 12-01	SUN 5-35 MERC. (R) 14-41		

MOON ASCDT.		JUPT.	
	Navamsa		RAHU
SAT. KETU			SUN
	MARS	VENUS	MARS

Whenever the nature of death is described as due to "displeasure of the sovereign" it includes all modern methods of execution, not necessarily being put on the stake which is now impossible. It can also include death by lynching in societies or States where law permits it. In a broad sense it covers all forms of unnatural death involving violence.

When a planet owning a malefic house or a functional malefic is in a Dustana, the Bhava represented by the Dustana is advanced. When the 8th lord is in any sign, the Bhava represented by that sign is impaired.

The 8th lord Sun in Chart 28 is in the 7th, the house of marriage. As head of one of the most revered *mutts* of the country, the native is a celibate monk. The 7th house position of the 8th lord has denied him marriage.

The 12th house is the last of the Dustanas and shows misfortune, wanderings, conjugal life (शयनसुख), expenditure and waste of wealth (वित्तक्षयं).

When the 12th house is in a moveable sign or is occupied by a Dustana lord (the 6th or the 8th lord), or is in conjunction with or aspected by Saturn, one may have to travel extensively.

Chart 28 : Born 18-7-1935 at 7-00 p.m. at 10 N 40, 79 E 29 with a balance of 0 years 4 months 6 days of Mars Dasa at birth.

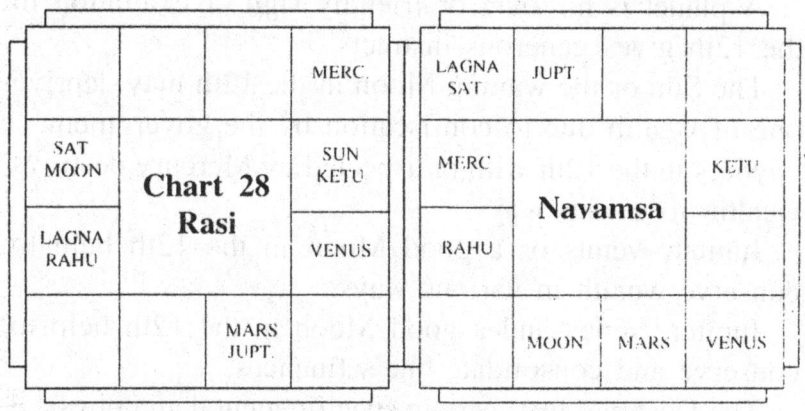

When a planet in the 12th is a benefic and is also aspected by a benefic, while the 12th lord is weak or occupies an inimical or debility sign, one will not have to spend his wealth.

When the planet in the 12th is weak but the 12th lord is strong, one will waste his money. Cases of wrong investments can also be included in this category.

When the 12th lord occupies benefic Vargas, then one will spend only on legitimate expenses.

When the 12th lord is weak or aspected by a weak planet, then one's expenses may be on questionable objects.

When a malefic 6th or 8th lord occupies the 12th in strength, one will loss his agricultural holdings and financial status.

A benefic in the 12th in a very general sense makes one liberal, virtuous and engage in agricultural or other simple and honest pursuits.

A malefic in the 12th makes one capricious, suffer from eye disease and flatulence, while at the same time making one restless and roving.

A planet is his own or friendly sign or exaltation in the 12th gives generous instincts.

The Sun or the waning Moon in the 12th may deprive one of wealth due to confiscation by the government.

Mars in the 12th with or aspected by Mercury destroys wealth in various ways.

Jupiter, Venus or a good Moon in the 12th help to conserve wealth in various ways.

Jupiter, Venus and a good Moon in the 12th help to conserve and consolidate one's finances.

The Dustanas give certain specific mental and physical deficiencies under certain conditions.

If the Moon conjoined with Mars is in the 6th, 8th or 12th, one is shameless.

If the 4th or 9th lord is in the 6th, one is dishonest and deceitful (कपटी).

If the 8th lord is in the 4th, then also one is dishonest.

A thieving mentality is shown by the 12th lord in the 3rd or the 4th lord in the 6th or the 8th lord in the 2nd or by Mars and Mercury being in the 6th.

The 12th lord in depression gives one a vulnerability to addictions. Malefics in the 12th make one viciously disposed as also unlucky.

The 12th house being primarily concerned with expenditure, certain specific combinations point to drainage or decimation of money through different sources.

Mercury in the 12th shows loss through litigation with brothers and cousins.

A malefic in the 12th can show black money.

If the Lagna lord is not strong, the 2nd lord joins the Sun in the 12th, loss of wealth is through criminal courts.

The 11th lord in the 12th, the 12th lord in the 2nd and the 2nd lord in a Dustana or in debility bring in loss through criminal proceedings.

The 2nd lord and 12th lord exchanging houses and the 1st lord in the 6th conjoining malefics show waste of wealth through criminal cases.

If the ruler of the sign occupied by the 2nd lord in Navamsa is in conjunction with a malefic and in a Dustana — the 6th, the 8th or the 12th — aspected by the Lagna lord, loss through theft, fire etc. is foreseen.

The 12th lord weak and conjoining Gulika or a malefic and related to the 6th lord shows destruction of wealth through enemies.

If such 12th lord conjoins the 7th lord, the loss of wealth is through one's wife; if Mars, through brother; if the 5th lord, through sons; if the 10th lord, through the father; and if the 4th lord, mother.

If the 12th house has more of malefic aspect, there is frequent or recurring loss of money.

If the Sun conjoins Rahu and Venus in the 12th, the expenditure is through fines and courts.

If the 12th house has Jupiter, it will be through tolls and taxes.

If the waning Moon and Sun are in the 12th, wealth is confiscated by the government.

If Mars and Saturn are in the 12th, expenditure is through brothers.

The Lagna lord in the 12th, malefics in the 2nd and the 10th lord conjoined or aspected by the 11th lord shows heavy debts.

The Lagna lord conjoined by a malefic and with or aspected by 6th, 8th or 12th lord also shows debts.

The Lagna lord in the 6th, 8th or 12th joined by the 2nd lord and the 9th unaspected by benefics also gives debts.

A Parivartana between the Lagna and Dustana lords brings in some adverse results. If the Lagna and 6th lord exchange signs, one will be free from disease, brave and powerful. If it is with the 8th lord, one is a gambler and trickster. If the exchange is with the 12th lord, one is despised, miserly and devoid of intelligence.

Good results associated with the 12th house are connected with visiting shrines and pilgrimages.

Chapter 7

Good and Bad Results from Dustanas

7

CERTAIN UNUSUAL situations that one rarely encounters in life, and more especially in society today such as ostracism are shown by malefics occupying the 6th, 8th or 12th from the Ascendant or the Ascendant lord. Likewise, heavy afflictions to the 10th house or 10th lord from the Dustana lords, in particulr, the 8th lord can also lead to such ostracism as in the case of being barred from taking examinations or holding certain offices or playing a certain sport.

Chart 29 is of an Indian cricket captain who was banned for life from playing the game following allegations of match-fixing in 2000.

Chart 29 : Born 8-2-1963 at 10-25 p.m. at 12 N 22, 78 E 26 with a balance of 2 years 1 month 23 days of Mercury Dasa at birth.

			RAHU 6-45 MARS (R) 21-23
JUPT. 25-07	**Chart 29** **Rasi**		MOON 28-19
SUN 27-20 SAT 22-34 KETU 6-45			
VENUS 11-14			ASCDT. 27-29

	MOON KETU		JUPT.
			VENUS SAT
	Navamsa		
	MERC MARS		ASCDT. RAHU SUN

The Vargottama Ascendant and benefic Venus in the 4th with Digbala took the native to the top in his cricket career. Though born in humble circumstances, he was able to achieve a high degree of success as also affluence. However, the afflictions to the 10th lord Mercury from the 6th lord Saturn, 12th lord Sun and more particularly, retrograde 8th lord Mars, led the native into circumstances leading to humliation and a ban from playing the game again.

When the 6th, 8th or 12th house is occupied or aspected by benefics with their rulers being in good houses, strong, exaltation or own signs Astra, Asura and Musala Yogas are produced.

The 6th house Yoga, Astra, makes one vanquish one's powerful enemies but makes one rude and arrogant in behaviour, with bruised limbs but strong body. One will be quarrelsome.

The 8th house Yoga called Asura Yoga is evil — one will spoil other's work and become a tale-bearer. He will be intent on securing his own interests. He will be poor with forbidden cravings, will do mean acts and be troubled by the effects of his own actions (स्वयंकृतानर्थपरंपरार्तं:).

The 12th house Yoga is Musala and one born in it will be the owner of wealth earned with much difficulty; he will suffer humiliation, his wealth will be steady, he will spend on good causes, will be foolish and fickle-minded and is said to go to heaven after death.

If the lords of the 1st to the 12th Bhavas starting from Lagna onwards occupy the 6th, the 8th or the 12th associated with or aspected by a malefics, 12 kinds of Yogas are formed with almost always adverse results, except in 3 cases.

If the 2nd lord is in a Dustans, Nisva Yoga is produced. He will be foul tongued, have a barren wife, have wicked friends, dental and eye troubles, will be stupid and will be robbed of his wealth by enemies.

If the 3rd lord is in a Dustana, it is a Mriti Yoga which leads to defeat by one's enemies, absence of brothers, makes one shameless, weak and without wealth, easily excited and bent on doing bad deeds.

Kuhu Yoga is caused by the 4th lord in the 6th, 8th or 12th. This makes one bereft of mother, vehicles, friends, happiness, ornaments and relations, without a house or even losing one's house and fond of low female company.

Pamara Yoga arises if the 5th lord is in a Dustana and makes one foolish and wretched. One will lie, cheat, lose children, be gluttonous, atheistic and fond of bad company.

The 6th lord in the 6th, the 8th or the 12th is a Harsha Yoga with good results such as happiness, enjoyment, good health and strength, God-fearing and virtuously inclined, with influential friends.

The 7th lord in a Dustana is Dushkriti Yoga when one loses one's wife or husband and is addicted to other's wives or husbands, is a vagabond, suffers from venereal and other such diseases and problems from the government. One's relatives despise one.

The 8th lord in a Dustans causes Sarala Yoga when one becomes long-lived, fearless, prosperous and endowed with scholarship, childern, riches. One achieves success in one's undertakings, overcomes his foes and becomes a celebrity.

Nirbhaya Yoga is formed by the 9th lord being relegated to the Dustanas. One loses all paternal property, despises elders and becomes irreligious. Shabby in dress, one will be reduced to indigence.

The 10th lord in the 6th, 8th or 12th causes Duryoga when whatever one does ends in failure. Scoffed at by all, one will be treacherous, selfish and a glutton. One may wander aimlessly.

The 11th lord in a Dustana leads to Daridra Yoga where one gets crushed under debts, becomes cruel, suffers from ear-troubles, get cought in criminal or anit-social activity, is a liar and becomes servile.

The 12th lord in a Dustana forms a Vimala Yoga which makes one spend little. A good-natured person, one will be happy, independent, known for his good qualities and in a noble profession.

If Venus, Mercury and Jupiter are in the 8th, Asura Yoga is formed (**JA** II-26). Any one of these planets is also capable of producing this Yoga but then, the results will be proportionately diluted.

Chart 30 : Born 22-9-1959 at 08-07 p.m. (IST) at 10 N 29, 79 E 20 with a balance of 1 month 2 days of Sun Dasa at birth.

KETU	LAGNA	MOON	
	Chart 30 Rasi		
			VENUS
SAT.	JUPT.		SUN RAHU MARS MERC.

SUN MOON	MERC. RAHU		MARS VENUS SAT.
	Navamsa		LAGNA
			JUPT.
		KETU	

The 8th house is occupied by Jupiter in Chart 30 giving rise to an Asura Yoga. The native is very cruel, abusive and violent. He flies into a rage at the slightest and uses the most obnoxious words to show his anger. His wife and children live in perpetual dread of the native who regularly beats them with a belt. Otherwise, for all practical purposes, he has a good job overseas and is seen as an excellent man in his workplace.

Another example of Asura Yoga is of the widow (Chart 31) of the now dead Phillipines President. The

Chart 31: Born 2-7-1929 at 2-34 p.m. (ZST) at 14 N 35, 120 E 59 with a balance of 17 years 6 months 29 days of Venus Dasa at birth.

	MOON RAHU	MERC. JUPT. VENUS	SUN		SUN	JUPT	LAGNA SAT.	MARS KETU
	Chart 31 Rasi					**Navamsa**		
			MARS		VENUS			MOON
SAT. (R)		KETU LAGNA			RAHU			MERC.

native's obsessive love for the good things of life, vicious temper, greed, avarice and arrogance are only too well-known.

According to **Jatakalankara**, II-26,

रन्ध्रस्थानस्थिता वा स्थिरभवनगता: शुक्रवागीशसौम्या: ।
कृच्छ्रणां कर्मणां ना भवति हि नियतं कारकस्तद्भाव:॥

If Venus, Mercury and Jupiter are in the 8th or in fixed signs, one will necessarily have to do very hard or painful duties. One will be hard hearted in disposition. This is particularly so where the Ascendant is afflicted and weak.

While Mercury, Venus and Jupiter are held to be adverse in the 8th, Jupiter in the 6th, Mercury in the 8th and Venus in the 12th are said to be even desirable.

The interchange of Dustanas by their lords gives rise to what is known as Vipareeta Raja Yoga. For example, the 6th lord in the 8th, the 8th lord in the 12th and the 12th lord in the 6th can cause this Yoga. The maleficience of all the lords gets diffused and highly favorable results are produced resulting in swift and sudden elevation in career, prosperity and success in everything one does. Very often, it leads to a very high office.

When the 6th, 8th and 12th lords occupy Kendras or Trikonas in strength while the 1st, 10th, 4th and 9th lords are weak and eclipsed and in Dustanas, then Duryogas are generated which damage the potential of the chart for good results to a major degree. But if these same Dustana lords are well-placed and the 1st, 4th, 10th and 9th lords are also well-placed in a Kendra or Trikona, the native becomes fortunate, successful, happy and wealthy.

Therefore, while the Dustanas are a reference to the evil houses, the results associated with Dustanas can be good or bad, depending upon how they are occupied and where their lords are placed. *(00-2001)*

Chapter 8

Understanding Rahu and Ketu

RAHU AND KETU are described as Chayagrahas or shadowy planets in astrological works. The orbits of the Sun and Moon around the earth intersect at two points. The North Point is known as the North Node or Rahu. The descending point which is exactly 180^0 away from Rahu is called the South Node or Ketu. Being points, these Nodes have no mass and are not visible to the human eye unlike the other Grahas – the Sun, Moon, Mars, Mercury, Jupiter, Venus and Saturn. Nevertheless, Rahu and Ketu are often the most impactful in influencing results. Understanding in what ways Rahu and Ketu show up in the chart in terms of events or happenings is easily one of the most difficult tasks encountered by an astrology student.

Rahu is often described as giving results akin to Saturn according to the dictum *Sanivad Rahu.* Saturn is clandestine, clammy and secretive. But Rahu sometimes acts just the opposite. He can be explosive, incendiary and confrontist.

Ketu is said to give results similar to Mars – *Kujavad Ketu.* If Mars is argumentative, Ketu is repressive. How do we reconcile these often contradictory and confusing features of the Nodes ?

Rahu covers a wide variety of significations and **Uttarakalamrita** gives a big list of these. Beginning with something as inconsequential as *umbrella,* the following including *kingdom* come under Rahu.

Gathering, fallacious arguments, speech that is vexatious, low caste, wicked female, decorated vehicle, irreligious man, gambling, strength at twilight, intrigue with wicked female, going to a foreign country, impurity, bone, spleen enlargement, falsehood, downward look, perplexity emerald, facing the South, recourse to low caste people or outcastes, bad swelling (ulcerous or infected or even cancerous), big forest, moving in rugged places, mountain, pain, staying outside, inclined towards Southwest, wind, phelgm, sorrow, serpent, night breeeze, severe, long, reptile, reading of dreams, travel, Muhurtha, old age, vehicle, world of serpents, mother, father or maternal grandfather, air, acute or sharp pain, catarrh, breathing, great prowess, forest, worship of Goddess Durga, wickedness, cohabitation with quadrupeds, writing of *krura bhasha* (Urdu according to some interpretations) and harsh speech.

In many ways, Rahu is the anti-thesis of accepted norms, conventionality and tradition. Rahu dominant in the 7th house or related to 7th house factors often results in unconventional marriage.

When Rahu Dasa is about to commence, especially in the case of teenagers, they become uncontrollable, rebellious and sometimes, even wayward.

If Rahu is related to the 5th house, his Dasa tends to lead one into addictions, the degree of affliction to the 5th house and to the Lagna and the Moon deciding the nature and extent of addiction.

Rahu in the 5th can give both very good and very poor results relating to education. If Mercury is well-placed then Rahu if related to the 5th and such a Karaka suddenly thrusts educational distinction on a native after which there is no turning back. If Mercury and the 5th house are otherwise ill-placed, Rahu obstructs educational opportunities and affects academic performance due to sudden loss of concentration, great restlessness or even through going astray.

Rahu with the Moon often leads to schizophrenics or split personalities. If Mercury also join the combination, the result is clouded thinking and a paranoid. One constantly harbours the suspicion others are after him and out to get him or victimise him at different levels of existence — domestic, vocational and other.

Rahu in the 10th aspected by Saturn and Venus and with the Moon receiving only malefic influences (at any rate with no benefic influence) gives excessive avarice and greed and makes for a kleptomaniac. Such natives often covet others' belongings and at the first opportunity, coolly flick them without any qualms. They may, for all practical purposes, appear normal in other ways and cover even family members, religiously inclined housewives and even otherwise good friends.

Rahu in the 9th afflicted makes one a typical fanatic in outlook. While it tends to generate a cunning, cruel, aggrandising mentality, it makes one mouth the holiest of holy words. Such people are experts at cheating others, while at the same time expecting total submission to them. The affliction gets more pronounced if the afflicting planets are Mars and Saturn. This combination in some form or the other, occurs in charts of so-called godmen whose secret activities and lives have generated shocking scandals. If Venus joins the Rahu-afflicted planetarium in the 9th house, then the scandal will involve girls and women.

Rahu joining the 10th house without affliction offers excellent career opportunities, sometimes even taking the native overseas.

Rahu in the 10th usually endows one with innovative genius and such natives, whatever their field of activity, discover or blaze a new path.

Jagadish Chandra Bose has Rahu in the 10th and he was the first to show the world plants wince when hurt and bloom better when patted with love and spoken to with kindness. Mahatma Gandhi had Rahu in the 10th in Cancer and working for the uplift of the downtrodden masses of India, he set out on the path of non-violence to wage a relentless fight for Indian Independence. The Mahatma's approach was hitherto unknown in the national life of any country. Sri Ramakrishna Paramahamsa's life too was of a totally different kind. His search for Divinity did not estrange him from his consort whom he looked upon as the Divine Mother Herself.

Rahu in the 3rd, 6th, 9th or 11th generally promotes material fortune. Alone here, Rahu can confer undiluted happiness and prosperity.

Rahu in the 2nd, though good for financial success, sometimes can generally cause monetary difficulties and is not easy to understand in Dhana Bhava. But Rahu here is sure to mar domestic peace by internal bickerings, dominating relatives, exploiting and opportunistic in-laws and burdensome responsibilities on the home front. Rahu in this house may impose on the native caring for and tending aged or sick relatives too.

Rahu in the 4th is disastrous for married life. It can create friction and suspicion between the couple due to a spineless spouse and a dominating, even wicked mother-in-law. Siblings of the spouse also contribute to the native's misery and domestic strife. If the Karaka Venus or the 7th house is also afflicted, then the spouse can be unfaithful causing great pain to the native. If the 8th house is afflicted and Rahu is in the 4th, Rahu Dasa can show loss of spouse by death.

Rahu in the 5th house gives results of differing nature depending upon the signification involved.

The 5th house shows deep-seated cravings and hidden appetites (urges). Rahu in the 5th or with the 5th lord, unless there are benefic influences, leads one to develop some kind of addiction or the other. It can also be infatuation for one beyond one's reach. This could imply one could get involved with a married man or woman but later come to distress on account of rejection by such persons.

Chart 32 : Born 31-12-1959 at 4-10 p.m. (IST) at 28N43, 77E47 with a balance of 9 years 9 months 28 days of Moon Dasa at birth.

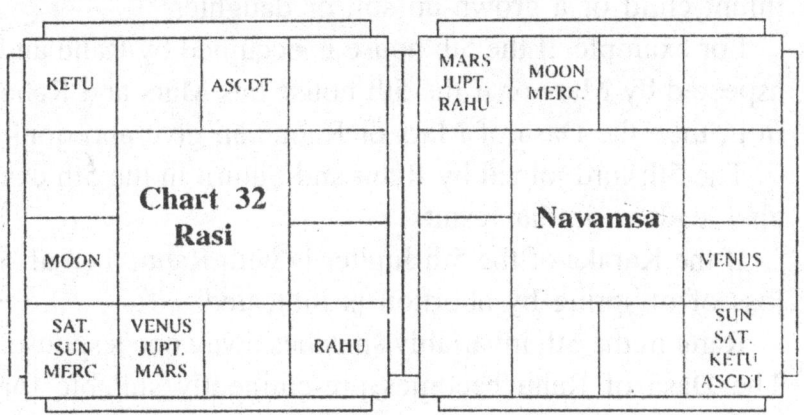

Rahu occupies the 5th house aspected by Saturn in Chart 32. In Saturn Bhukti of Rahu Dasa, the girl got drawn to a young man. But two years later, the friendship broke off leaving the native depressed. Though Karaka Venus is quite well-placed, Rahu in the 5th did not help the involvement culminate in marriage.

The Moon Bhukti again saw her fall in love with a colleague, a married man with children. The man is not likely to give up his family and children for the girl.

Rahu in the 5th house is of particular significance in matters related to progeny. It usually signifies difficulty in begetting issue or suffering and anguish due to or on account of issue.

If Rahu occupies the 5th house or is aspected by Mars or if the 5th house is a sign ruled by Mars with Rahu there, one suffers distress on account of loss of progeny.

If Mars influences the 5th house occupied by Rahu by aspect, occupation or in other ways, then usually, unless there are other benefic influences, there is loss of issue. Depending upon the Dasas, the loss may take the form of abortion or miscarriage or still-birth or even death of infant child or a grown-up son or daughter.

For example, if the 5th house is occupied by Rahu and aspected by Mars or if the 5th house has Mars and Rahu in it, then the Dasa of Mars or Rahu can give abortions.

The 5th lord joined by Rahu and Saturn in the 5th can also lead to similar results.

If the Karaka of the 5th Jupiter is with Rahu, then also loss of offspring by abortion is indicated.

Rahu in the 8th invariably snatches away one's spouse. The Dasa of Rahu becomes pre-eminently suitable for such a tragedy; otherwise, Rahu Bhukti in the Dasa of any other appropriately placed planet can cause the damage.

Rahu in the 7th is usually a puzzle. Rahu can generate high voltage marital tension in this house. Or else, he can give marriage with an uncle's son or daughter and happiness in marriage. Rahu in this position can also suggest a non-conformist marriage or an elopement. A strong tendency to marry outside one's religious caste, community or even race is prominent in such cases.

Rahu in the 1st is not too bad. It can make for a diplomatic shrewd personality. If afflicted by Mars or Saturn, such natives become dangerous, manipulative, cruel, avaricious, even fanatical. An affliction-free Moon or well-placed Lagna lord tones down these traits considerably.

If Rahu should occupy the 12th, it is to be viewed with caution. It can show sexual perversions, promiscuousness and criminal inclinations. If the planet afflicted by Rahu in the 12th is the Sun, the native becomes a pauper, losing all his paternal inheritance. He is vulnerable to be duped by conmen. If the 12th is further afflicted, he can become a cheat himself, tricking others, embezzling and misappropriating other's money.

The Moon afflicted in the 12th by Rahu makes for a dangerous personality that is murderously suspicious and often involved in smuggling and other clandestine or illegal activity. Such people either kill or commit suicide if other afflictions are also present.

Mercury in the 12th afflicted by Rahu produces confidence tricksters who are sophisticated, dressed well and with an appearance and manner that is deceptively impressive. The area of operation of such natives is usually finance. Violent crime is not their forte. Street-smart, resourceful and ingenious, they operate with slickness.

Mars in the 12th house with Rahu is a dreadful combination to have. Such a native is sucked, against his will and under the force of powerful circumstances, into the vortex of crime, drug-traffic and more particularly, prostitution.

Jupiter in the 12th house with Rahu causes one to squander money on vices. The emphasis here in more on weaknesses of the flesh than crime.

If Rahu is joined by Venus in the 12th house, he pollutes the conjugal life of the native. The spouse may seek gratification outside the marriage. In some cases, the Venus-Rahu combine gives sublimation of the libido and the attainment of the highest level of spirituality.

Saturn and Rahu in the 12th lead to base perversions, frigidity and unhealthy company.

Chart 33 : Born 20-9-1934 at 2-10 p.m. (CET) at 40N52, 14E16 with a balance of 3 years 9 months of Mars Dasa at birth.

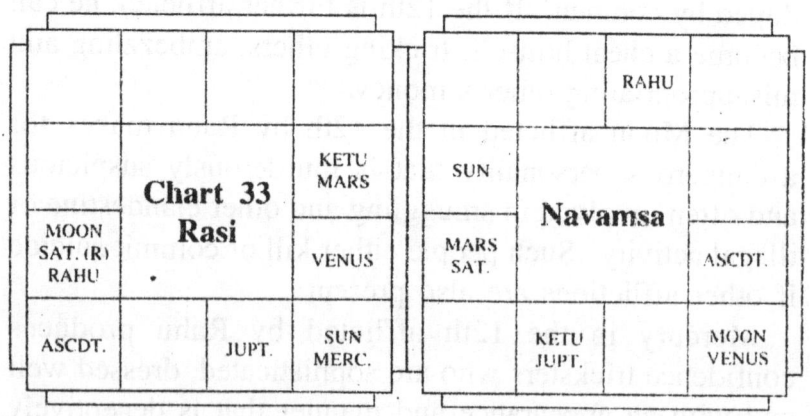

Rahu is said to give the results of his sign-dispositer in his Dasa. This is more so if Rahu is alone and not joined by any other planet.

If Rahu associates with any other planet, he gives results pertaining to that planet, and of course, the results of Saturn also. For example, if Rahu is with a benefic planet, he gives favorable results in his Dasa. If the planet he joins is a malefic, the results too would not be happy.

The native of Chart 33 was born in indigent circumstances. The father never married the native's mother but went away leaving the woman to bring up her two daughters during the war. The little girl's was an impoverished childhood. She was thin and always hungry. The balance of Dasa at birth was 3 years and 9 months of Mars.

Rahu, whose Dasa came next, is with the 2nd lord Saturn and with 8th lord Moon aspected by 12th (and 5th) lord Mars, which explains her difficult days as a little girl. Rahu with the Moon and Saturn chose to give the results of the 8th lord Moon. The Moon as 8th lord is not benefic.

In the 15th year of her life, the girl who had now grown up into an attractive and elegant young woman won a beauty contest. This was in Venus Bhukti of Rahu Dasa. Venus is the Asuraguru and Rahu is a demonical Graha. Therefore, in charts that have the potential, Venus Bhukti in Rahu Dasa can generate trends that reorient the entire chart. The beauty title brought her a film contract and after that, there was no turning back. She went on to become an international star and celebrity.

Most of Rahu Dasa (the first twelve years) was far from happy. Rahu reflected the results of the 8th lord

Moon until the Bhukti of Venus pushed Rahu to change over to giving the results of Saturn *(Sanivad Rahu)*, the 2nd lord. As long as Rahu gave the results of the 8th lord Moon, he was bad. But once he switched over to reflecting Saturn's results, he became helpful and even favorable, as Saturn here is the the 2nd lord occupying his own sign Capricorn and in Vargottama strength generating good finances.

Likewise, Ketu gives the results of his sign-dispositer if alone and to some extent, of Mars as well. If associated with any planets, he gives their results, malefic or benefic, depending upon the rulership of the planet.

Chart 34 : Born 1-10-1924 at 7-22 a.m. (LMT) at 32N02, 84W24 with a balance of 13 year 14 days of Jupiter Dasa at birth.

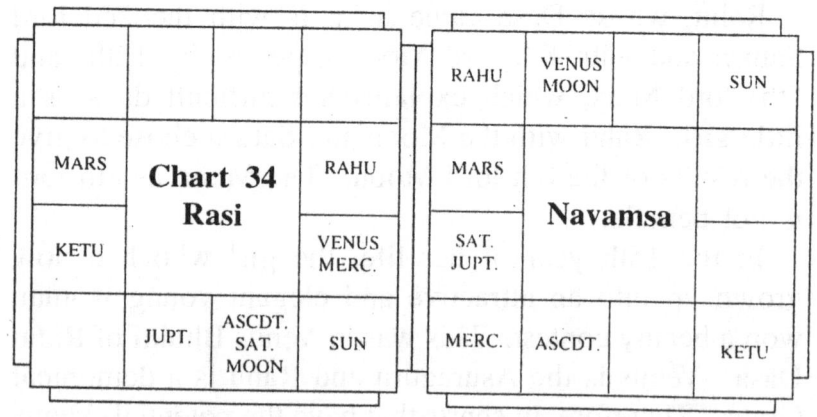

The native of Chart 34 became President of the United States of America in 1976 in Ketu Dasa. Ketu is in the 4th with no other planet. Ketu occupies a Saturnine sign and Saturn is a Yogakaraka both from Lagna and Chandra Lagna. Saturn is exalted and aspects the 10th. Saturn also joins the 10th lord Moon.

If Ketu associates with any planet, he reflects the results that planet would give. For an Aquarius birth Ascendant, Ketu with Mercury in the 8th gave a good academic career. In Ketu Dasa, further academic qualification at the post graduate level came with distinction.

Ketu has a number of significations and the **Uttarakalamrita** gives a comprehensive list of these. Ketu shows worship of Chandesha, Ganesha and other forms of God, doctor, dog, cock, vulture, salvation, all kinds of wealth, consumption, pain, fever, bath in the Ganges, great penance, wind, hunter, friendship, conferring of prosperity, stone, wound, the science of witchcraft, inconstancy, knowledge of Brahman, belly, eye-pain, stupidity, thorn, deer, knowledge, vow of silence, philosophy, all kinds of luxury, luck, trouble from enemies, poor eater, indifference to the world, paternal grandfather, hunger, intense pain in the stomach, boil or such other affliction, horned creature, servant of Siva, revoking the order of arrest and company of menial workers and labour class.

Chapter 9

Planets and Palliatives

THE SEER attitude of the Vedantic sage is hardly compatible with the operation of free-will. But here and there strewn in classical Vedantic literature, one finds thoughts that destiny is not all inexorable.

जन्तूनां नरजन्म दुर्लभमतः पुंस्त्वं ततो विप्रता
तस्माद्वैदिक-धर्ममार्गपरता विद्वत्वमस्मात्परम् ।
आत्मानात्मविवेचनं स्वनुभवो ब्रह्मात्मना संस्थितिः
मुक्तिर्नौ शतकोटिजन्मसु कृतैः पुण्यैर्विना लभ्यते ॥

Part of this Sloka, read as a corollary, means that it is only through the result of good deeds that a human birth is acquired. If you look at it more deeply, it also reiterates the law of Karma or rebirth and the scope of free-will.

The law of Karma is not stifling — one gets only what one sows. Yet, it provides options and allows room for the operation of free-will. In other words, it provides a system where action of a kind, though in the process of bearing results, can be manoeuvred into relatively less impactful effects. That is, a certain consequence though bound to result out of a certain action can be suitably amended to lose its sting. Not all causes attract this discount. Some do. Others don't. Yet, others come only partly under this relief. Remedial measures are a concomitant of this system.

As in law where there compoundable and non-compundable offences, so also do we have planetary afflictions (Arishtas or Doshas) that are amenable to Shantis (palliatives) and those that are not.

A horoscope carries many features some of which are indelibly stamped on the native's rendezvous with life. The Lagna (Ascendant), the Moon and Mercury severely afflicted give serious physical, mental and psychological deficiencies, economic difficulties and personal problems of a grave kind. All these come under the category of *Prarabdha Karma* the results of which must be borne patiently until they exhaust themselves.

In other cases, a strong Ascendant or the Moon can make up for certain other drawbacks in the chart. In such a case, the problem becomes amenable to solution, but mostly because of the native's persistence and perseverance. Jupiter's aspect or association is a sure indication that the natal deficiency can be set right or at least sufficiently ameliorated. As the 5th and 9th lord, his aspect on the afflictions makes remedies easily available. Once properly sought and carried out, all that the native has to do is to wait for the results. As the 3rd, 6th, 8th and 11th or a quadrangular lord, although palliatives may not be lacking, the native may face problems in resorting to them in the prescribed manner and the results may be only partial or may get unduly delayed. Any trinal lord, for that matter, influencing the Dosha-causing (affecting) planets allows room for hope and human effort. Malefics as the 6th, 8th and 12th lords and with additional afflictions may not yield even to remedial measures. Patience and endurance are the only ways out. Sometimes, a very weak Moon or Ascendant also acts to block out solutions inspite of benefic aspects. In such instances, either the natives or people who have a say in their lives, tend to be obstinate and fool-hardly shutting out all hope.

We are reminded, in this context, of one of the 19th century rulers of Mysore. The period was just before the British deposed the king for alleged maladministration. The royal astrologers were distressed by certain planetary configurations in the king's horoscope foreboding his fall from power. They got together and after a series of deliberations, discovered certain *danas* (giving away in charity certain prescribed articles) could act as a palliative and prevent the downfall of the king. A very important requirement of this remedy was to get someone truly worthy of receiving the gift. After a hard search spread over the entire country, they found a pious Brahmin called Somayaji in one of the villages in a remote corner of the State. He was known for his severe austerities and had for years been a *Surya-upasaka* (one who propitiates the Sun). The Maharaja's counsellors, in accordance with the advice of the astrologers, invited Somayaji to visit the court of the Mysore king and receive the onerous *danas* meant to prevent the evil forebodings.

The appointed day found the gentle Brahmin before the king ready to receive the *danas*. But the courtiers and the people gathered there to witness the momentous *dana* were stunned to see the Brahmin stretch out his left hand for the *arghya* (water meant to signify the change in ownership of the article offered as *dana* which the king had to offer. In our country, the left hand does not enjoy the same status as the right hand and is to be used only for certain functions. Handing something with the left hand is deemed to be a sign of contempt. How could this poverty-stricken man be so arrognat, they wondered. Once they got over their excitement, the courtiers rushed to where the Brahmin stood and prevailed upon him to stretch out his right hand in accordance with etiquette and tradition. With a bemused look, Somayaji held out his right palm. No sooner did the water drops trickle on to his palm through the golden *uddharana* (traditional spoon) they evaporated at once. Only now did the wisemen of the court realise their folly in trying to make the Brahmin adhere to etiquette. Being a *Surya-upasaka*, he was bristling with the heat of penance and knowing well his right hand could burn away the essence of the *dana*, he had put forth his left hand. But destiny had willed it otherwise. The remedy (*dana*) was destroyed before it could be accepted. The inevitable and tragic fall of the kingdom followed inspite of the best astrological advice.

Planetary afflictions can be resolved through three commonly known means. They are through the use of an appropriate precious stone (*mani*), prayers and incantations (*mantra*) and medication (*aushadha*).

Medication is commonly known but it applies mostly to physical ailments and only rarely, and that too only unsuccessfully, to mental and nervous disorders.

It is a common belief that precious stones, carefully chosen, can indeed work miracles. But semi-precious stones as advertised by most jewellers are of no use astrologically. The planets rule over the *navaratnas* or the nine gems. The Sun governs the ruby (*manikyam*), the

Moon the pearl (*mouktikam*), Mars the coral (*vidrumam*), Mercury the emerald (*marakatam*), Jupiter the lapiz lazauli (*pushyaragam*), Venus the diamond (*vajram*), Saturn the sapphire (*neelam*), Rahu the cat's eye (*gomedham*) and Ketu, the agate (*vaiduryam*). Afflictions that can be ascribed to a particular planet are said to be allayed by the appropriate stone. Cases of eye problems have responded to the use of a good quality ruby. There have been several instances of mental and other kinds of stress that are usually the result of jaundiced emotions being allayed with the proper use of quality pearls. It tends to make one less at war with oneself and also others.

A peep into the exhaustive treatise from Kerala, **Prasna Marga** (*vide* English translation by Dr. B.V. Raman) gives innumerable ways of identifying the afflicting planet and of locating the right remedy. All problems are traced to one's sins of commission or omission. Remedies consist of medicines, Japas (repetition of Mantras), Homas (oblations), worship, gifts, feeding and several other kinds. The *Mahamrityunjaya Mantra* is extolled as the best of remedies and is universal in application. Mental and psychic ailments come under control by its Japa, Homa and feeding the poor in the prescribed manner. The presiding deity is Lord Siva under whose domain comes *Sani* or Saturn. All problems that can be attributed to Saturnine influence, in particular, of transit or direction, can be effectively curbed or even removed by this Japa.

In the case of a young lady (Chart 35), the first sign that there was something wrong with her was noticed when she began to blabber foul words with intermittent fever that upset all her career and other plans. This state of affairs continued for more than a month. On premonition, her brother went up the roof of the house where he found a bamboo doll in female attire with jute strings around its neck. The family of the girl suspected she was a victim of black magic (*kshudra vidya*) which indeed she was as is evident from the affliction to the 5th house by Saturn and Rahu and also from the eclipsed Moon.

Chart 35 : Born 1-8-1956 at 6-35 a.m. (IST) at 13 N, 77 35' E with a balance of 3 years 5 months 9 days of Sun Dasa at birth.

MARS		MOON KETU	VENUS	MERC.	KETU		
	Chart 35 Rasi		ASCDT. SUN MERC.		**Navamsa**		JUPT. MARS
				ASCDT. MOON MANDI			SAT.
			JUPT.				
	SAT. RAHU	MANDI		SUN	VENUS	RAHU	

The Dasa on was of Rahu afflicting the 5th house indicating lack of *poorvapunya* leaving little doubt that the malady of the girl had psychic roots. Rahu with Saturn and the Nodal axis across the 11th and 5th houses suggested the trouble had been caused by paternal relations. (The Moon is afflicted by Dasa lord Rahu and Saturn, the 11th lord from the 9th while the Moon is in the 3rd from the 9th indicative of co-borns of the girl's father as having engineered the spell). But it should be noted that the 9th is occupied by the 5th lord Mars in the constellation of the 9th lord. This gives strength to the chart as a whole so that appropriate remedial measures can be expected to effectively check and even destroy the trouble-causing forces. The *Maha Mrityunjaya Japa* and Homa were performed in the prescribed manner and soon the lady was her bright, chirpy normal self.

How does prayer work as a remedy ? When one prays one puts one's ego (which is synonymous with duality) to rest and supplicates the Universal Self for grace. It is only too well-known that all human ills (*Tapatrayas*) are the result of the ego. When the little self or ego is subdued, it allows for our true nature to function. Our true nature is but Divinity and Divinity means the end of all problems springing from duality. In practice, when most of us pray, there still remain traces of the ego which refuses to be subdued completely and in proportion do our afflictions fade away or remain.

The subject of appropriate remedies through the propitiation of deities could well nigh run into an encyclopaedic volume. But, the principal forms of the one Supreme are sufficient for any kind of problems. The Sun, the Mother Goddess, Lord Subrahmanya, Maha Vishnu, Maha Vishnu, the Mother Goddess again, Lord Siva, Lord Siva and Ganapati govern respectively the Sun, Moon, Mars, Mercury, Jupiter, Venus, Saturn, Rahu and Ketu. Rahu gives results akin to Saturn's and it would be quite logical to bring the former too under Lord Siva. While the *Sahasranama* (the thousand names) of Vishnu and Amba (Mother Goddess) are popular, Siva is best prayed for through the *Maha Mrityunjaya Mantra*. Ganapati's grace is sought through His *Ashtottari*

(108 names) and Subrahmanya's through visiting his shrines. The Sun is brought to one's aid through the *Aditya Hridayam*. These are easy to practise but even then, they must be first learnt from a qualified personage so that the very little *niyama* (regulations) that goes with them is scrupulously followed.

There is another kind of palliative that is both easy and difficult at the same time. Where relations are involved, it behoves on the astrologer to infuse hope and confidence in the native to stick on to his guns until the directional influences change for the better.

In the case of an estranged couple, their charts indicated that the marriage would get straightened out in a couple of months. Perhaps, the stress of separation must have taken its toll of the young man for he began to entertain suspicions of his wife's character. At this point of time, the most sensible remedy around was to present the relevant features of the wife's chart to the young man in such a manner as to allay his worst fears. This in

Chart 36 : Female : Born 20-4-1955 at 9-20 a.m. (IST) at 23N 27, 77 E 13 with a balance of 3 years 5 months 11 days of Ketu Dasa at birth.

	SUN MERC.	VENUS KETU	ASCDT.	JUPT. (R)	MARS		KETU MOON SUN
MARS	Chart 36 Rasi		JUPT. (R)		Navamsa		VENUS
			MOON				
	SAT. (R) RAHU				RAHU	ASCDT. MERC.	SAT. (R)

itself acted as a palliative to pull himself together without resorting to any impulsive action.

The Lagna in the wife's case (Chart 36) is Gemini and its lord is in the 11th with the 3rd lord. This association indicates a warm and friendly nature but not of a flirtatious kind. The 7th lord Jupiter occupies his exaltation sign aspected by the 6th lord Mars. This together with the Subhakartari Yoga (being hemmed in between 2 benefics) to which the Lagna is subject to is a Sahacharya Yoga or a combination that shows fidelity. This combination was highlighted and a Mantric remedy suggested. Since the male chart (Chart 37) was under the influence of the

Chart 37 : Male : Born 21-5-1951 at 11- 50 a.m. (IST) with a balance of 19 years 6 months 0 days of Venus Dasa at birth.

	SUN MERC. JUPT. MARS				VENUS SUN	JUPT.	ASCDT. RAHU	
VENUS								
	Chart 37 Rasi		KETU		MERC.	Navamsa		MARS
RAHU			ASCDT. MOON					MOON
			SAT. (R)			KETU		SAT. (R)

Moon Dasa, the Moon being a female planet and the problem being one coming under the Karakattwa (signification) of Venus, another feminine planet, a daily racital of *Lalita Sahasranama* resulted in the couple making up and coming together. In such cases, counselling in carefully chosen words can be a very effective remedy when considered from the purely common-sense angle.

What reiterated the lady's chastity was not only the planetary dispositions in her own chart but also the 7th house in the young man's chart. His Venus, though in a dual sign, was exalted and even if aspected by a natural malefic Saturn, came under his influence as the 7th lord primarily. The 7th house and lord are under the influence of Jupiter. Jupiter's role here indicates Divine Grace and the efficacy of human prayer.

Astrology is a science of correlations. Planets, or to use the more appropriate word *Grahas*, do not cause events. Planetary movements and happenings on this earth are related by a law of synchronicity. With this background, how can palliatives be admitted on the scene ? If from a horoscope, one finds Mercury as the culprit behind a certain affliction and that propitiating him would help, what exactly is one talking about ? If Mercury's position in the chart does not have a cause and effect relationship with the sorrows of the native and is only a correlation, how can propitiating him influence the events in the native's life ? When one talks of Mercury in this context, one is talking not about the planet, the physical body orbiting the skies, but about a living, feeling deified force that has control over all matters ascribed to the astrological Mercury. The grossest manifestation of this force is that inert physical mass found always close to the Sun while his most subtle bearings are anchored in the Universal Soul.

The ancient sages of India who knew the limitations of the sensory organs, through some other means of perception, must have discovered that the Cosmic Power was filtered into various grades of delegation, each presiding over certain cosmic forces and Karmic laws of a particular kind. In order to invoke these cosmic nominees to get them to favor them with relief or reward, the same sages must have discovered or evolved methods all coming under the general term of "remedial measures". Each nominee was referred to by the name of the planet which must have been his grossest manifestation. It could be that these nominees together were entrusted with the entire system of Karmic laws, each being further entrusted with a particular set or group of these laws. Further, each of them must have been empowered to condone deserving cases on application. This application could take the form of remedial measures handed over to us by the sages.

When a particular problem is ascribed to a particlar planetary affliction, it could be due to the transgression of a Karmic law coming within the jurisdiction of the nominee whose grosser form is the physical planet found responsible in the chart. A palliative to this planet is prescribed. What actually happens is that the prayer or remedial measure is addressed or directed to the nominee in-charge of the Karma in question. When his grace descends, relief appears.

The whole system of remedial measures could have been founded on this theory. That this theory works in practice could also be sufficient evidence of its validity as a law.

The role of the afflicting planet is akin to the cardiogram graph. The graph does not rule the heart-beats but only registers them. When it turns faulty, one appeals to the doctor-in-charge, not to the graph.

Nevertheless, the graph is indispensable and gives a clue to the condition of the heart. So also the planets. They register events under the Karmic laws and when one suffers, one finds a corresponding affliction in the chart. An appeal (*Shanti*) is made to the nominee-in-charge to help one out of the Karmic abyss. The mode and kind of appeal is determined on the basis of the planetary juxtapositions, just as the ups and downs of the graph determine what course of action is to be taken next.

Some sort of a Cosmic Computer must be in operation programmed to match individual Karmas with planetary movements. This computer, one is tempted to believe, at the exact moment when an individual destiny pattern is in consonance with a particular set of planetary combinations and permutations triggers off the birth of the individual on *terra-firma*. (09-'85)

Chapter 10

Notes on Gulika and Mandi

Chapter 10

Notes on *sulka* and Mind

THE NAVAGRAHAS — the Sun, Moon, Mars, Mercury, Jupiter, Venus, Saturn, Rahu and Ketu — are nine in number. Of these, Rahu and Ketu, though on par with the seven visible and physical entities from the Sun to Saturn, are in some ways, not full-fledged Grahas. For example, they can claim no ownership over any of the Zodiacal signs. Nor do they have clearly defined areas of exaltation, Moolatrikona, own or even inimical signs. Their status is somewhat akin to nomads. They are in a very general sense, equated with the major malefics — Rahu with Saturn and Ketu with Mars. Rahu and Ketu are known as Chayagrahas because they have no physical mass and are elusive to the eye and the senses. They are points of inter-section of the orbits of the Sun and the Moon. Therefore, these Nodes otherwise are dependent on the luminaries. To that extent, the so-called Upagrahas are similar to the Nodes in as much as they are also based on the position of the luminary Sun at a particular point of time. The Upagrahas are 5 in number — Dhooma, Vyateepata, Parivesha, Indrachapa and Ketu (not the same as the South Node). Their positions are derived from that of the Sun.

Sun's logitude *plus* 4s 13° 20' gives Dhooma.

12 signs *minus* Dhooma gives Vyateepata.

Vyateepata *plus* 6 signs gives Parivesha.

Again, 12 signs *minus* Parivesha gives Indrachapa. Indrachapa *plus* 16° 40' gives Ketu.

All these Upagrahas are broadly classed as malefic and inauspicious सर्व कर्म विनाशक: (*Sarvakarmavinasakah*).

These Upagrahas in combination with the Sun, Moon or the Ascendant are said to cause destruction of the family, longevity and wisdom (वंशायुर्ज्ञान नाशकम्).

Apart from these 5 Upagrahas, Gulika is the most commonly known one. So also Mandi. But no one seems to be sure if they are two different Upagrahas or if both mean the same.

दिवसानष्टधा कृत्वा वारेशाद् क्रमात् ॥११॥
अष्टमांशो निरीश: स्यान्छन्यंशो गुलिक: स्मृत: ।
रात्रिम्यष्टधा कृत्वा वारेशात् पञ्चमादित: ॥१२॥
गणयेदष्टम: खण्डो निरीश: परिकीर्तित: ।
शन्यंशो गुलिक: प्रोक्तो गुर्वंशो यमघण्डक: ॥१३॥
भौमांशो मृत्युरादिष्टो रव्यंश: कालसंज्ञक:।
सौम्यांशोर्धप्रहरक: स्व स्वदेशोद् भव: स्फुट: ॥१४॥

According to **Brihat Parasara Hora** (Chapter IV), the duration of day is divided by 8. The lord of the 1st part is the lord of the weekday in question and the lords of the remaining parts are the rulers of the weekdays following in that order. The Sun is the ruler of the 1st part on Sunday. The 2nd part is ruled by the Moon, the 3rd by Mars, the 4th by Mercury, the 5th by Jupiter, the 6th by Venus and the 7th by Saturn respectively. The 8th part has no ruler. The part ruled by Saturn is called Gulika.

For night times, the duration of night is divided into 8 equal parts. The first part is ruled by the ruler of the 5th day from the weekday in question, the other parts upto including the 7th being ruled by the planets in continuing order from the 5th weekday lord. For example, on a Sunday night, the first part is ruled not by the Sun as for a day-brith but by the ruler of the 5th weekday from Sunday, namely, Jupiter, the 2nd part by Venus, the 3rd by Saturn, the 4th by the Sun, the 5th by the Moon, the 6th by Mars, the 7th by Mercury and the 8th is deemed as having no ruler. Saturn's position comes under Gulika. (Chapter IV)

The part ruled by the Sun is called Kalavela, that by Jupiter is Yamaghantaka, that by Mars is Mrityu while the part ruled by Mercury is called Ardhaprahara.

Gulika is deemed a malefic. Parasara does not seem to differentiate him from Mandi. At places, he uses Mandi for Gulika and *vice-versa*.

Results of Gulika in the 12 houses, according to Parasara, are :

First : Afflicted by diseases, lustful, sinful, crafty, vicious and very miserable.

Second : Ugly or *Vikrutah*, miserable, mean, given to vices, shameless and penniless.

Third : Charming in appearance, head of a village, virtuous, liked by good people, honoured by the ruler.

Fourth : Sickly (*Rogi*), unhappy, always engaged in evil (sinful) deeds (सदा पापकृता) and afflicted by bilious and gastric disorders.

Fifth : Insignificant, poor, short-lived, mean and spiteful, eunuch, hen-pecked and atheist.

Sixth : Invincible, robust physique and sturdy limbs, brilliant, beloved of one's spouse, optimistic, endowed with fortitude and of a helpful nature.

Seventh : Unhappy in marriage, given to evil deeds, debauchee, having no friends and living off his wife.

Eighth : Starving, miserable, cruel, wrathful, wicked, poor and with no good quality.

Ninth : Many hardships, emaciated, doing evil deeds, dull and a tale-bearer.

Tenth : Many sons, happy, enjoyments, pious and God-fearing, righteous life.

Eleventh : Fond of aristocratic ladies, leader, working for the welfare of relatives, short and ruler of men.

Twelfth : Engaged in vile deeds or occupation, sinful, physical deformity in limb, lethargic and drawn to base female company.

These results are subject to the effects of the other nine planets on the chart as a whole.

A careful examination of these results will show that Gulika acts as any other natural malefic would. He is malefic in the 1st, 2nd, 4th, 5th, 7th, 8th, 9th and 12th while good in the 3rd, 6th, 10th and 11th houses.

Jataka Parijata gives 9 Upagrahas for the Navagrahas in Chapter II, Sloka 6 :

क्रमशः कालपरिधिधूमाधूमार्द्धप्रहराह्वयाः ।
यमकंटककोदण्डमान्दिपतीपकेतवः ॥

For the Sun, Kala; for the Moon, Paridhi; for Mars, Dhooma; for Mercury, Aradhaprahara; for Jupiter, Yamakantaka; for Venus, Kodanda; for Saturn, Mandi; for Rahu, Pata and for Ketu, Upaketu are the Upagrahas or secondary planets.

Jataka Parijata gives similar results to Gulika as **Brihat Parasara Hora Sastra** and also looks at Gulika's association with malefics in some houses. Gulika is at some places, referred to as Mandi leading one to infer that Vaidyanatha Dikshitar does not treat the two as distinct entities. He says in Chapter IX, Sloka 1 :

．．．． मान्द्यब्दादिफलानि वच्मि गुलिके लग्नस्थिते ॥

That, he is considering the effects of *Mandiadi Grahas* and goes on to give the results of Gulika in different houses. From Sloka 2 onwards, he uses the term 'Mandi' in different ways such as *Mandasuta, Mandaja. Mandaputra, Manda* etc., not Gulika.

Gulika's association with a malefic in the 1st house is said to make one deceitful, lustful and depraved. In the 2nd house, one has no wealth or even a semblance to education and learning (विद्याविहीन).

There are also other results attributed to Gulika such as when in the :

Third House : He makes the person stand out due to his aloofness, pride, conceit and such qualities. He will be highly ill-tempered and very busy with the acquisition of wealth. He will be free from distress and will be without brothers and sisters.

Fourth House : The person will be bereft of Vidya, Dhana, Griha, happiness, lands and vehicles and will become a wanderer.

Fifth House : The person will be immoral, irresolute, evil-minded, with few sons and short-lived.

Sixth House : Will destroy hosts of foes, will be interested in black magic and similar occult pursuits and be brave.

Seventh House : He will be quarrelsome, have a bad wife, inimical to many people (could be anti-social), stupid and ungrateful.

Eighth House : Will be deformed in his face, with weak eyes and of weak body.

Ninth House : Will be engaged in vile deeds and may even kill his parents and preceptors.

Tenth House : Will give up or disregard all duties and obligations of his caste, status and relationship; and will have no self-respect.

Eleventh House : Much happiness, wealth, power and beauty, but will lose elder brother.

Twelfth House : Will move around giving the impression of an ascetic and will be able to extract money from others through his powers of speech.

Gulika's association with different Karakas does not help the significations.

With the *Sun* — will hate his father; with the *Moon* — will cause distress to mother; with *Mars* — will have no younger brother; with *Mercury* — will be insane; with *Jupiter* — a heretic; with *Venus* — venereal diseases and a profligate; with *Saturn* — fond of pleasure and enjoyment; with *Rahu* — poisoner; and with *Ketu* — incendiary (militant, terrorist).

When in a house affected by Vishanadi — even if born a ruler, one is said to become a beggar. This disposition of Gulika is treated as so damning as capable of destroying everything in the native's life.

Major planets associated with Gulika are said to produce malefic results.

Gulika with the Karaka tends to taint the Karakattwa much in the same manner as any other malefic would. For example, Gulika with Mars who is the Karaka for brothers is said to deprive one of younger siblings. Although this result may not literally occur in every chart that has a Mars-Gulika combination, it could take the form of lack of happiness (a) from younger siblings; or (b) on account of younger siblings; or (c) because of their absence. Just as Venus would be afflicted by Saturn, Mars, Rahu or Ketu, likewise does Gulika act on the Kalatrakaraka, depriving the native of happiness from spouse. However, what emerges from a careful appraisal of the results attributed to Gulika in different houses is that the negative result generated may be of a very base or mean nature. For example, Gulika with the Sun could give such petty and mean differences between the native and his father, one would be ashamed to talk about them. Nevertheless, they would be such as to create in the mind of the native, distinct hatred for the father.

Gulika may be said to represent all that is vulgar, base, sordid and disgusting, and therefore, his association with any planet may bring out these qualities in the relationship or situation concerned.

While most classical texts detail out results attributed to Gulika's occupation of different houses, there is another school of thought that prefers to believe that Gulika's Drishti (look) or aspect alone is harmful and not, his occupation. This astrological truth is presented in the form of a story.

Ravana, the King of Lanka, after he was granted the boon of near-immortality by Lord Brahma, went about conquering different Lokas. About this time, his wife Queen Mandodari became heavy with child. Ravana was worried about this child and about what kind of a destiny it would carry with it. He, therefore, resolved to ensure his unborn babe would be invincible and perfect in all ways. When the date of delivery began to draw close, Ravana caught hold of all the planets, bound them together and drove them into a single Zodiacal house so that they would lead to the birth of an invincible king of kings. The planets, right from the Sun to Saturn, were helpless and bound as they were by Ravana, waited restlessly for the birth of the child so that they could then go free. Saturn, as we all know, is the most distant planet, cold and shivering. The Sun is the ruler of the solar system and radiant with the brilliance of his great heat and energy. Saturn tied up with the Sun was the most afflicted. Used to staying away in an orbit remote from the Sun, this proximity to the blazing planet, was more than he could bear. Hot, stuffy and uncomfortable, poor Saturn began to perspire profusely. As the perspiration began to run down his face, Saturn began to get more and more uncomfortable. With his long ugly nails, he scratched his face and the dirt on it with the tiny rivulets of perspiration came out in the form of a small globule or Gulika. Ravana continued to keep a close watch on the planets, lest they shift ever so slightly and change their positions to thwart his plans. Afraid Ravana would notice his fidgeting Saturn rolled up the scum into a ball and threw it off. Ravana noticed this movement of Saturn and at once struck him on the leg. Poor Saturn was left a cripple. But, luckily the gods had seen the globule fly

Creator, to breathe life into it. Even as Brahma invested it with Prana and the globule landed in a section of the Zodiac, the babe was born. As he grew up, the child shone like the Sun himself and was more handsome than anyone else. He was brave, valiant, intelligent and the envy of all. But, unfortunately the moment of his birth got blemished by Gulika landing at a point in the Zodiac which led to a severe curtailment of longevity.

This child, Indrajit as he was later called, was destined to have a short life. When Ravana found out what had happened, he was furious. He caught hold of Gulika and tied him face down to the steps of his throne. Each day as he went up and down the steps of his throne, he trampled on him. Gulika's agony was unbearable but the planets could do little to help him. It fell on the great Sage Narada to help him out. Narada knew Gulika had this important property of destroying whatever he looked at. The sage went up to Ravana and taunted him saying he was doing a very un-Kshatriya-like thing in keeping Gulika bound face down and trampling him on his back. A Kshatriya should face his enemy. "Turn Gulika round so that he can see the splendour of your throne and then trample upon him", said Narada to Ravana.

Ravana was intoxicated with the pride of his conquests and learning. He did not stop to ponder over what Narada had told him. He ordered his men to turn Gulika over. He then trampled upon this hapless Upagraha and even as he did so, Gulika's gaze, filled with the venom of hate at the humiliation he had been subject to, fell on Ravana. And, with this, began the events that led to Ravana's ultimate defeat and death.

Gulika in short, acts as a mean malefic.

Chapter 11

More Notes on Gulika and Mandi

Chapter 11

More Notes on Gulbin and Hand

GULIKA IS said to rise during the one-eighth part of the day (or night) coming under Saturn. For day-births, the rulers of the one-eighth parts start with the ruler of the weekday in question, followed sequentially by the successive weekday lords with the 8th part having no ruler. For night-births, the first one-eighth part is ruled by the ruler of the 5th day from the weekday in question, the other parts being ruled, as in day-births, by the weekday lords in sequential order from the 5th weekday lord onwards. Gulika or the part ruled by Saturn can stretch over an hour and more, and therefore, can cover sometimes, one sign and sometimes, two signs. Which of these, in the latter case, is to be shown as Gulka ? **The Gulika Sphuta or longitude of Gulika is that rising on the Eastern horizon at the point of time when Saturn's one-eighth part commences.**

Example (Chart 38) **:** Born on 24-10-1949 (Monday) at 3-33 p.m. at 13 N, 77 E 35.

Sunrise	=	5-50 a.m. (LMT)
Sunset	=	17 h. 13m. (LMT)
Duration of day	=	Sunset − Sunrise
		17h. 33m. − 5h. 50m.
Duration of day	=	11h. 43m.
Dividing it by 8, we get	=	$\frac{11h.\ 43m.}{8}$ = $\frac{703m.}{8}$
	=	87·875m.

Therefore, each one-eighth part of the day = 87·875 minutes.

Since the weekday in question is a Monday, the first one-eighth part is ruled by the Moon, the second by the Mars, the 3rd, 4th, 5th, 6th and 7th by Mercury, Jupiter, Venus, Saturn and the Sun respectively, the eighth part having no ruler. The one-eighth part ruled by Saturn is called Gulika.

Saturn's part begins at 439·375 minutes (= 7h.19·375 m.) after sunrise.

Saturn's part ends at 527·25 minutes after sunrise.

Therefore, Saurn's part begins at 5h. 50m.
+ 7h. 19·375m.
─────────
=13h.09·375m. (LMT)

Gulika rises at = 13h. 9·375m (LMT)
= 13h. 29m. 7s. (IST)

Therefore, Gulika = Capricorn 21^0 34'.

According to **Sarvartha Chintamani**, Gulika and Mandi are two different entities. Gulika is said to be *Sanisuta* or the son of Saturn. Mandi, on the other hand, is described as *Yamatmaja*, son of Yama and called Pranahara (snatcher or destroyer of life) and Atipapi (exceedingly sinful). Mandi is said to be fearful and ugly, eccentric and fitful, generally fond of evil deeds and low company. In fact, Mandi as also Ketu, the Node (not Upaketu), are said to represent all lower castes.

Mandi is said to show localities of death and execution. He also rules dirty clothes, iron, lead and other metallic ores.

In birth or lost horoscopes, or even in Prasna, especially relating to lost objects, Mandi is assigned 18 months.

Mandi becomes important, especially in cases of doubtful Lagna. Mandi's calculation is quite different from Gulika's

Mandi rises at the end of 26 Ghatis*, 22 Ghatis, 18 Ghatis, 14 Ghatis, 10 Ghatis, 6 Ghatis and 2 Ghatis from sunrise on Sunday, Monday through Saturday respectively. This is for obtaining the position of Mandi during day-time. For getting Mandi's position during night-time, we have to calculate the sign rising at 10, 6, 2, 26, 22, 18 and 14 Ghatis respectively for each of the weekdays starting from Sunday onwards.

Mandi for Chart 38 works out to $321° 3'$ or Aquarius $21° 3'$.

Chart 38: Born 24-10-1949 at 3-33 p.m. (IST) at 13N, 77E35 with a balance of 3 years 3 months 18 days of Saturn Dasa at birth.

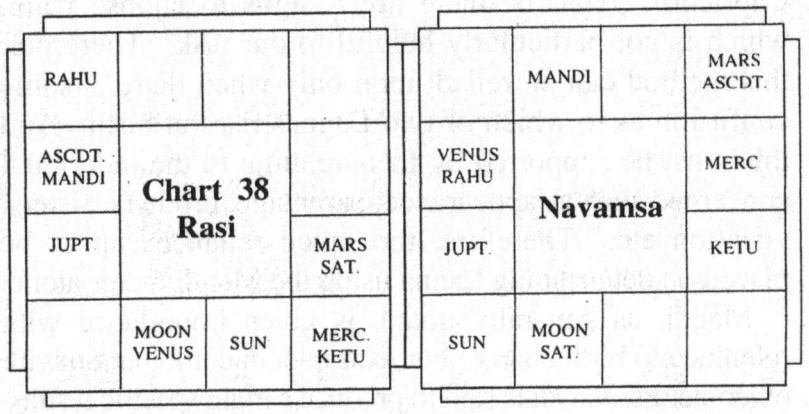

---

* 60 Ghatis = 24 hours
  1 Ghati = 24 minutes

According to **Sarwartha Chintamani**, when the Prasna or birth-Lagna is doubtful, fix (1) the 5th or the 9th from the Navamsa occupied by Mandi, or (2) the 5th or 9th from the 7th from the Navamsa occupied by Mandi, or (3) the 5th or 9th from the Navamsa occupied by the Moon, or (4) the 5th or the 9th from the 7th from the Navamsa occupied by the Moon, as Lagna.

Accordingly, we make a note of the factors listed as qualifying for Lagna in Chart 38.

(1) Mandi is in Aries Navamsa. The 5th and 9th from it are Leo and Sagittarius.

(2) The 7th from Mandi in Navamsa is Libra. The 5th and 9th from it are Aquarius and Gemini.

(3) Pisces and Scorpio are the 5th and 9th from the Moon in Navamsa.

(4) The 7th from the Moon is Taurus. The 5th and 9th from it are Virgo and Capricorn.

Therefore, the Lagna may be any one of Leo, Sagittarius, Aquarius, Gemini, Pisces, Scorpio, Virgo or Capricorn. That is, there are 8 signs to choose from, which is not particularly helpful to our task. Therefore, this method can be relied upon only when there is some confusion as to which of two Lagnas rises at birth. And this must be supported by facts relating to the individual concerned such as appearance, parentage, brothers, sisters, vocation etc. Therefore, too much reliance cannot be placed on determining Lagna using the Mandi factor alone.

Mandi, as generally noted, is given importance with reference to birth charts. For example, in combination with other factors, Mandi is said to produce certain specific results.

A birth occurring when a malefic is in Lagna and Gulika in conjunction with a Kendra lord in a trine (Trikona) is said to bring evil to the person born.

If Rahu is in Lagna, Gulika is in a trine and Mars *cum* Mandi are in a Kendra, testicle enlargement is indicated. Such combinations imply the two are different entities.

Likewise, if the ruler of the Navamsa occupied by the Lagna lord joins Rahu, Mandi and Mars, one's testicles will be swollen.

If the 3rd lord joins Saturn or Mandi, brothers die.

If there is a malefic in the 3rd joined by Mandi, a neck disease of a virulent type is shown.

In the case* of Sri Ramakrishna Paramahamsa (Chart 39), there is Mandi in the 3rd house aspected by Mars and Saturn, both natural malefics but exalted. The Paramahamsa was stricken by throat cancer. Although the exact combination is not present here, Mandi in the 3rd is afflicted by retrograde Saturn's aspect.

Chart 39 : Born 18-2-1836 at 6-23 a.m. at 22 N 53, 87 E 44 with a balance of 12 years 1 month 6 days of Jupiter Dasa at birth.

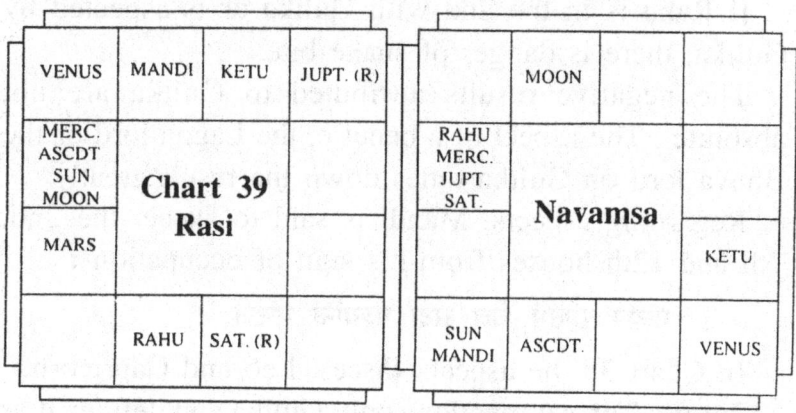

Mandi is in a fiery malefic Nakshatra Krittika ruled by the Sun who afflicts the Lagna with the 6th lord Moon

---

* **Notable Horoscopes** by Dr. B.V. Raman, page 160.

rendering it vulnerable to a terminal disease. The locus of the disease as shown by Mandi is the throat.

If Saturn joins the 3rd with Gulika and there is no aspect from benefics, there is danger from winds. (Possibly, this covers cases where property, limb or life is lost due to blizzards, cyclones, typhoons and wind-storms.)

If Rahu and Saturn combine in a cruel Amsa aspected by Gulika and if the 9th lord occupies cruel Amsas, one will be cold-hearted, inflicting suffering and injury on mankind and devoid of compassion.

If a weak 12th lord is joined or aspected by the 6th lord and combines with Rahu and Gulika, one loses money through enemies.

If the 12th house falls in evil or cruel Vargas and the 12th lord joins Saturn, Mandi or Rahu, there will be deformity in the body.

If Rahu is in the 2nd with Gulika or is aspected by Gulika, there is danger of snake bite.

The negative results attributed to Gulika are not absolute. The aspect of a benefic, the Lagna lord or the Bhava lord on Gulika tones down the result greatly.

Regarding aspects, Mandi is said to aspect the 2nd, 7th and 12th houses from his sign of occupation :

मध्येन सप्तमं चैव सदा पश्यन्ति मन्दजः

In Chart 38, he aspects Pisces, Leo and Capricorn.

Jataka Tattwa mentions only Gulika and defines it as rising at the end of the one-eighth part assigned to Saturn.

Gulika is condemned as predominantly evil but this is with reference only to the birth chart :

मन्दतमसी धर्मे गुलिकदृष्टेऽतिपापि । M–17

Saturn and Rahu in the 9th aspected by Gulika lead to sinful acts.

Malefics in the 4th and the 4th lord weak conjoined with Gulika is said to produce the same result :

यद्बद्धावीयरन्ध्रेशसूर्यशनिगुलिकेशगुलिकांशेशानां
मध्ये योऽधिकबली तत्पाके मूर्तिवित्तादिनाशः ॥ C - 8

In the case of any Bhava, find out who is the strongest of the lord of the 8th from the Bhava, the Sun, Saturn. lord of the sign occupied by Gulika and the lord of the Navamsa occupied by Gulika. In the Dasa of that planet, loss of beauty, wealth etc. may occur.

The Dosha or evil of Gulika is dealt with in great detail in **Kalaprakasika (KP)**. Here, the reference is clearly to Gulika and it is in connection with Muhurtha or elections.

Gulika along with the other Upagrahas is deemed inauspicious for Muhurtha or elections. But Gulika in the rising sign is rendered ineffective under certain conditions :

गुरूणा बलिना दृष्टे शुक्रेणाथ बुधेन च ॥२३॥
युक्तकांक्षितमुक्ताश्च गुलिकाद्याः शुभवहाः ।
शुक्रयोगे शुभं सर्वं जीवान्मुक्ति तथा शुभम् ॥२४॥

— **KP** Chap. 34

When aspected by powerful Jupiter, Venus or Mercury, the evil of Gulika vanishes. The aspect of or association with Venus converts all evil into good.

Usually, there is some reservation about accepting Abhijin Muhurtha on a Wednesday on the ground there is Gulika in Lagna. However, this feeling is not justified.

गुलिकोऽपि न दोषाय वारेशो वा विलग्नग: ।
शुभवारांशगे चन्द्रे लग्नगे बलसंयुते ॥२६॥
गुलिकोदयजं दोषं सद्य एव विनश्यति ।
शुक्रो वा सुरपूज्यो वा लग्नग: शुभवीक्षित: ॥२७॥
— KP Chap. 34

When the ruler of the weekday is well-dignified or in the rising sign, the adverse effect of Gulika need not be considered. Gulika in the Ascendant produces no harm, when powerful Moon occupies the rising sign in a benefic Navamsa or in that of the lord of the weekday. Jupiter or Venus in Lagna aspected by benefics nullify its evil effects. Even this condition is redundant because according to **Jataka Madhaveeyam**, अभिजन् सर्वदोषज्ञ: or Abhijin Muhurtha renders all Doshas ineffective and Gulika in Lagna is not a major or Maha Dosha.

धान्यसंग्रहमभ्यङ्गं लवनंक्रयविक्रयम् ॥२८॥
नयनोन्मीलनं श्राद्धं भूषणं ऋणमोक्षणम् ।
अग्न्याधानं प्रवेशश्च गन्धलेपनभेषजे ॥२९॥
गजाश्वारोहणं मन्त्रस्वीकारञ्चोभिषेचनम् ।
आभिचारं महादानं वेदारंभम् विशेषत: ॥३०॥
विंशतिञ्चाचरेद्बिद्धान्विशेषद्गुलिकोदये ।
केन्द्रत्रिकोणयो: सौम्यैस्त्रिषडायगता: परे ॥३१॥
— KP Chap. 34

Gulika in Lagna is not always unfavorable. He is favorable for certain kinds of activities such as harvesting and in-gathering of corn, oil bath, trade, carving the eyes of a deity, death anniversary rites, ornamentation, paying off debts, worshipping fire, opening ceremony, perfuming oneself, medical treatment, initiation, black magic, for giving away land (in charity) and study of the **Vedas**.

केन्द्रेगे सुरनाथेऽच्चे शुक्रे वा विष्टिनाशनम्
षष्ठयष्टमीकृतं दोषं गुलिकोदयमेव च ।

— **KP** Chap. 34-48

Jupiter or Venus well-degnified in a quadrant radically thwarts the evil effects of Vishti, Gulika in the rising sign, Shashti, Ashtami and the last days of the dark fortnight produce no harm when Jupiter is posited in a quadrant.

Prasna Marga refers to Mandi as Gulika at several places and the method of determination of Mandi is the same as in other classical treatises. Whenever the author refers to Gulika in this text, it is to be taken as meaning Mandi.

There are copious references to Mandi, especially in timing death.

Death can occur when :

(a) Saturn transits the sign held by Mandi or its trines for a day-birth.

(b) Saturn transits the 7th from Mandi or its trines for a night-birth.

In Chart 38, the birth being during day-time, death can occur when Saturn transits either Gemini, Libra or Aquarius. Since the chart is a Poornayu chart (as per standard methods of Ayurdaya), death can take place when Saturn transits Libra, that is, just when the 3rd round of *sadesathe* or Saturn's seven-and-a-half year transit is about to begin.

Pramana Gulika helps narrow down the time-frame further. For a day-birth, the position of Gulika on the previous night *plus* 180° gives Pramana Gulika. For a night-birth, the position of Gulika during day-time is the Pramana Gulika.

Death is said to occur when :

(1) Saturn passes through the Rasi occupied by Pramana Gulika ;

(2) Jupiter passes through the sign occupied by the Navamsa lord of Pramana Gulika ;

(3) The Sun passes through the Rasi occupied by the lord of the Dwadasamsa occupied by Pramana Gulika; and

(4) The Moon passes through the Rasi occupied by the ruler of the Trimsamsa in which Pramana Gulika is placed.

In Chart 38, the birth occurs during day-time. Therefore, the position of Mandi (referred to as Gulika in **Prasna Marga** worked out for the same date but taking the time as for night (23/24-10-1949 at 3-33 p.m. IST) is to be taken for determining Pramana Gulika.

Mandi = $70°\ 39'$
Therefore, Pramana Gulika = $70°\ 39' + 180° = 250°\ 39'$
Pramana Gulika = $10°\ 39'$ Sagittarius.

Death can occur :

(a) When Saturn passes through the sign occupied by Pramana Gulika, that is, when it transits Sagittarius.

(b) When Jupiter passes through the sign occupied by the Navamsa lord of Pramana Gulika. The Navamsa of Pramana Gulika falls in Cancer whose lord Moon occupies Scorpio in Rasi. Jupiter's passage through Scorpio can be critical.

(c) Likewise, by determining when the Sun and the Moon transit the signs occupied by the respective lords of the Dwadasamsa of Trimsamsa occupied by Pramana Gulika, the month and date of the event can be attempted.

The Sun in the 7th from Mandi in Navamsa shows death due to royal displeasure or अर्विपते:. Such a death can be through hanging, execution or lethal injection in cases condemned to death by the judiciary. It can also cover death by a firing squad which is still the practice in some West Asian and African countries when the rulers decide to dispense with an enemy. The weak Moon in the 7th from Mandi in Navamsa can cause death by drowning — while swimming or slipping into a well or cases of shipwreck. Mars leads to death on the battlefield and includes all forms of warfare — shooting, firing, biological gas etc. Saturn, the planet of intrigue and manipulation, bring about death through वञ्चना or deceit and betrayal. Rahu causes death by snake-bite and poisoning. While these results have been proved correct in several cases, one cannot jump to a conclusion only on the basis of one single planet in the 7th from Mandi in Navamsa. The aspects and associations of this planet must also be considered. But more importantly, we have to first examine the Rasi chart for the nature of death — violent or peaceful — and only then move on to Mandi in Navamsa for confirmation as well as for more specific details.

Saturn in Sarpa Drekanna or if associated with or aspected by Rahu or Mandi causes death by snake-bite. Saturn with Mars or the Sun in Aries, Leo or Scorpio if in an Agnibhuta Rasi (fiery sign) in association with or aspected by Rahu or Gulika is said to result in one being burnt to death. This combination can be tested in deaths due to fire accidents, bomb-blasts and even dowry death by burning. Saturn, weak and aspected or associated with Gulika or Rahu, if in a Kolemukha (the first Drekanna of Scorpio, Capricorn and Cancer) or a Pakshi Drekanna (the first Drekanna of Leo and Aquarius) causes death by being mauled by beasts or pecked by birds respectively.

Clues to the cause or agency of death can be found from the ruler of the sign occupied by Gulika. If such a ruler is heavily afflicted in the chart if the planet concerned is the Sun, it is the father; the Moon, the mother; Mars, brothers ; Mercury, relatives; Jupiter, the son: Venus, the wife (or husband); and Saturn, one's own self. If Saturn is the planet involved and otherwise heavily afflicted, then, it may be self-destruction or suicide. Here, it is the Karakattwas that are given as causing death. However, this rule may be safely adapted to include the lordships of the planets concerned also.

In Chart 40, Mandi occupies Scorpio in Rasi and Aquarius in Navamsa. The 7th house from Mandi in Navamsa is Leo occupied by Saturn and Jupiter. Saturn shows deceit or *Vanchana* as leading to the native's death. This apart, the Rasi chart has serious afflictions. Rahu and the Moon in the 8th are aspected by retrograde Saturn. Rahu-Moon-Saturn influences on the 8th show a violent end. The 7th lord Sun has Mandi aspecting it in Rasi and this can point to the husband as being the cause of death. In Navamsa, the Sun is in Lagna with Mandi. The Sun is the 7th lord, here too. The chart is of a woman who was supposed to have been bludgeoned to death by a blunt wooden object by her ex-husband. Saturn shows deceit and the Sun, by virtue of his lordship, rules the spouse. The heavy affliction to the 8th house in Rasi read with these clues from Mandi does justify the charge of murder against the deceased's ex-husband. These clues, if judiciously used, can be availed of to narrow down the

Chart 40 : Born 19-5-1959 at 2-00 a.m. (ZST) at 50 N 07, 8 E 40 with a balance of 5 years 1 month 23 days of Moon Dasa at birth.

KETU	MERC.	SUN	VENUS	VENUS		MOON	RAHU
ASCDT.		Chart 40 Rasi	MARS	SUN ASCDT. MANDI	Navamsa		MARS
							JUPT SAT.
SAT. (R)	JUPT (R) MA. DI		MOON RAHU	KETU			MERC.

suspects in cases of dowry and other deaths due to violence from relatives.

The position of Mandi can be used to trace different kinds of suffering in life. If Gulika occupies the Badhakastana, then one becomes vulnerable to torment from supernatural forces. Depending upon the position of Gulika and the planets he associates with, the supernatural force (disembodied soul) can be identified. For instance, if in the case of a man suffering torment of this kind if Gulika in the Badhaka house is in a sign owned by Mars or is otherwise associated with Mars, then it may be surmised that the trouble-causing soul is of a co-born who could have died a violent death and whose obsequies were not properly performed. Not only that, but whether if the departed soul died long back or recently as also its age at the time of death can be guaged by noting the nature of Rasi and Navamsa occupied by Gulika.

Gulika and Mandi seem to exchange and even share roles according to most classical works. These two Upagrahas are generally not taken into account while analysing a chart. Vasista, Gargi, Parasara, Vyasa, Varahamihira and other classical writers have not given much importance to Mandi and Gulika or even treated them as strictly distinct entities. Therefore, it would be in order to tow the line of these great masters. However, in cases where problems defy general principles of astrology or even common-sense, Mandi and Gulika provide some clues. In cases which are out of the ordinary and relate to afflictions caused by physical, mental, psychological or spiritual assault, these Upagrahas may be examined to narrow down the clues furnished by other planets. Mandi and Gulika are planets of a sleazy and sordid kind so correctly symbolised by the scum generated from the perspiration on Saturn's forehead. Naturally, they would be playing an important role in the charts of all shady and vulgar characters as well as victims of such people. Only an extensive study of such charts with emphasis on the positions of Mandi and Gulika would enable us to identify the degree and nature of their roles in horoscopy. This is an area that needs research based on a statistical study of cases.

Chapter 12

Combining Different Dasa Systems — Right or Wrong?

INTERPRETATION OF charts is a challenging job. It needs not only a thorough understanding of the theoretical part of astrology but also an ability to co-ordinate widely different, and sometimes even contradictory, factors into a cohesive synthesis that does not go against the realities of life even in the most unusual astrological circumstances. Hundreds upon hundreds of planetary combinations and permutations are available in classical works to cover almost every kind of event or situation that can occur in life. Likewise, transits and directional influences are treated in great detail to aid interpretation.

Ultimately, all these details have to be employed to explore one of two angles to the interpretation of a chart. One, is to see if a specific event is present in the chart. For example, marriage, child-birth, distinction, honour, career, accident, surgery, sickness, acquisition of money or land or whatever other event one may be interested in, should first be present in the chart and it should also be identified with a fair degree of definiteness. The second and the more difficult part of interpretation is timing the event. Usually, astrological tradition puts the optimum life span at the proverbial Shatayu or a hundred summers and within which period the event should be timed.

According to **Phaladeepika**,

नृणां द्वादशवत्सरा दशहता ह्यायुः प्रमाणं
परैरार्व्यातं परमं शनेस्त्रिभगणं यावत्परैरीरितम् ।
कैश्चिच्चन्द्रसहस्रदर्शनमिह प्रोक्तं कलौ किन्तु
यद्वेदोक्तं शरदः शतं हि परमायुदायमाचक्ष्महे ॥

XXII-26

*The full period of life in the case of men has been declared as 120 years (12 x 10) by some. Others there are who have stated that the full life-period is the time taken by Saturn to make 3 complete revolutions (in his orbit). There is a third school which says that the full life-period of a man is the time taken by the Moon for making 1000 revolutions. But we are of the opinion that the full period of man's life in this Kaliyuga is only 100 years as stated in the **Vedas**.*

Therefore, of the two angles involved in interpreting charts, the more challenging is easily the timing of the event and locating it in the time-frame of 100 years. For instance, if marriage is indicated at age 25, that would be perfectly comfortable. But what would be the situation if marriage is shown at 35 years or 47 years ? The latter two time-points would necessarily imply, especially, if it is a female chart, parental effort should not be confined to finding a suitable spouse but also consider academic and career opportunities with equal or even greater seriousness. Or, if a chart carries indications for begetting a child, what would be the interpretation if it is shown at say, the 24th or the 30th year ? And what would it mean if the event is scheduled astrologically, in the 70th year? In a female chart, it can only point to childlessness, leaving out the exceptional circumstances of medical experimentational techniques. Therefore, timing an event assumes great importance in understanding a chart. The Dasa system is precisely meant for timing events. **Brihat Parasara Hora** describes about 32 Dasa systems but the greatest importance is given to the Vimshottari Dasa system.

As Parasara says,

दशाबहुविधास्तासु मुख्या विंशोत्तरी मता ।
— Chap. 48-3

There are many kinds of Dasas but the most important is Vimshottari.

The Vimshottari Dasa system is explained by Parasara as follows :

कृत्तिकात: समारभ्य त्रिरावृत्य दशाधिपा: ।
आ-चं-कु-रा-गु-श-बु-के-शुपूर्वा विहगा: क्रमात् ॥१२॥
वह्निभाज्जन्मभं यावद् या संख्या नवतष्टिता ।
शेषाहशाधिपो ज्ञेयस्तमारभ्य दशां नयेत् ॥१३॥
विंशोत्तरशतं पूर्णमायु: पूर्वमुदाहृतम् ।
कलौविंशोत्तरी तस्माद् दशा मुख्य द्विजोत्तम ॥१४॥
— B.P.H. 40-12,13,14

The Dasa lords commencing from Krittika are successively the Sun, Moon, Mars, Rahu, Jupiter, Saturn, Mercury, Ketu and Venus in three cycles of Nakshatras. The number of Nakshatras between Krittika and the birth Nakshatra is to be divided by 9. The remainder indicates the Dasa lord reckoned from the Sun.

The full span of life is taken as 120 years (Poorna Ayus), and therefore, amongst the various Dasas, Vimshottari Dasa, which also is a cycle of 120 years, is deemed to be the prime Dasa system.

दशासमा: क्रमादेषां षड् दशाऽश्वा गजेन्दव:।
नृपाला नवचन्द्राश्च नगचन्द्रा नमा नखा :

— Chap. 40-15

The number of years assigned to each planet (lord of the Dasa) — the Sun, Moon, Mars, Rahu, Jupiter, Saturn, Mercury, Ketu and Venus — is 6, 10, 7, 18, 16, 19, 17, 7 and 20 respectively. The Dasa (at birth) is determined from the Nakshatra in which the Moon is in transit at the time of birth. This is the Janma Nakshatra.

In the Vimshottari Dasa system, the Nakshatra rulership follows a cyclic pattern with Aswini being ruled by Ketu, Bharani by Venus, Krittika by the Sun, Rohini by the Moon, Mrigasira by Mars, Aridra by Rahu, Punarvasu by Jupiter, Pushyami by Saturn and Aslesha by Mercury. The 27 Nakshatras of the Zodiac come under 3 cycles of 9 each with the planetary rulership repeating in the same order in all 3 cycles. This is a very important and distinguishing feature of the Vimshottari Dasa system. The Nakshatra rulerships assigned under it play a sensitive role in interpreting the chart and fine-tuning predictions.

The Vimshottari system is also called Udu Dasa, *Udu* meaning the Moon-based. But this sytem is not the only Nakshatra-based Dasa. There are several other Dasa systems based on the natal constellation such as Ashtottari

(100 years); Shodashottari (116 years); Dwadashottari (112 years); Panchottari (105 years); Shashtabdika (100 years); Chaturasiti Sama (चतुरशीतिसमा) (84 years) Dwisaptati Sama (द्विसप्तति समा) (72 years); Shashtihayani (षष्ठिहायनि) (60 years); and Shattrimshatisama (षट्त्रिंशतिसमा) (36 years).

The Ashtottari (108 years), according to Parasara, is to be applied under the specific condition of Rahu occupying a Kendra (quadrant) or Trikona (trine) from the Ascendant lord so long as Rahu is not in the Ascendant. That is, Rahu should occupy the 4th, the 7th, the 10th, the 5th or the 9th from the Ascendant lord for Ashtottari Dasa to be applicable.

If the Ascendant is Aquarius and its ruler Saturn is in the 7th in Leo, Rahu's position in any trine or Kendra from Leo (but other than Aquarius) would qualify the chart to come under the Ashtottari Dasa system. But if Rahu were to be in Aquarius, Pisces, Gemini, Virgo, Libra or Capricorn, then this Dasa system cannot be applied to the case.

Ashtottari can also be applied in cases of **day-births** occuring in the dark fortnight and of **night-births** occuring in the bright fortnight.

The Ashottari Dasa begins with the Sun Dasa starting from Aridra to Aslesha (both inclusive). The Moon Dasa next has rulership over Makha, Pubba and Uttara. Mars Dasa which follows the Moon again covers four Nakshatras—Hasta, Chitta, Swati and Visakha. Mercury Dasa comes next and covers the three succeeding stars —Anuradha, Jyeshta and Moola. Saturn Dasa, after that, again, holds sway over Poorvashada, Uttarashada, Abhijit and Sravana. The next Dasa of Jupiter rules Dhanishta, Satabhisha and Poorvabhadrapada. Rahu Dasa covers Revati, Uttarabhadrapada, Aswini and Bharani. Venus Dasa which follows Rahu covers Krittika, Rohini and Mrigasira bringing the cycle to an end. Each Nakshatra covers an arc of $13° 20'$ throughout except for Uttarashada whose arc is $10°$, Abhijit $4° 13' 20''$ and Sravana $12° 26' 40''$.

The Dasa periods, here, are different from Vimshottari and are for 6, 15, 8, 17, 10, 19, 12 and 21 years respectively for the Sun, Moon, Mars, Mercury, Saturn, Jupiter, Rahu and Venus. Ketu has no role in this Dasa scheme.

In the Ashtottari Dasa system, malefic planets get rulership over 4 Nakshatras and benefic, over 3 Nakshatras. Therefore, the Sun's Dasa of 6 years is divided over 4 Nakshatras, each getting 1·5 years or 18 months.

If, for example, the Moon occupies Anuradha Nakshatra at birth, the Dasa of Mercury would be current at birth under Ashtottari while under Vimshottari, it would be of Saturn who rules Anuradha. After Mercury Dasa, in the Ashtottari system, the native would pass through Saturn, Jupiter, Rahu, Venus, Sun, Moon and Mars Dasas in that order. As another example, if the Moon is in Aridra, then Rahu Dasa on at birth will be coloured by Rahu's position in the natal chart according to Vimshottari. But according to Ashtottari, as the Sun rules Aridra, Punarvasu, Pushya, Aslesha, the results of planets in these Nakshatras will be controlled by the Sun's position in the chart. The Moon in Aridra gives a Dasa balance which will be of the Sun and results will be based on the Sun's position in the horoscope. The picture can change totally. Such variance in interpretative details are a serious problem commonly encountered when different Dasa systems are applied to the same chart under the somewhat unreliable expectation of obtaining far better or more accurate results than by using Vimshottari alone *vis-a-vis* timing events.

Each of the other Nakshatra Dasas is to be applied under specific conditions. The order of the Dasas and the nature of their lords are quite different in each system.

Shodashottari Dasa is applicable when the Ascendant occupies the Moon's Hora in the dark fortnight. That is, the Ascendant should fall within the first 15° of even signs or the second half of odd signs and the birth should have occurred between Full Moon and New Moon. This Dasa system is to be applied also when the Ascendant occupies the Sun's Hora (the first 15 degrees of odd signs and the latter half of even signs) and the birth is in the bright fortnight (New Moon to Full Moon).

The Dasas are of the Sun, Mars, Jupiter, Saturn, Ketu, Moon, Mercury and Venus in that order with the Dasa periods being 11, 12, 13, 14, 15, 16, 17 and 18 years respectively. Rahu has no role here. The Janma Nakshatra is to be counted from Pushyami and this figure is to be divided by 8. The remainder gives the Dasa ruling at birth. For example, if Sravana is the birth star, it is the 15th counted from Pushyami. Dividing it by 8, we get quotient 1 *plus* remainder 7. The 7th Dasa counted in the order given above will be of Mercury and this will be in operation at birth to be followed by those of Venus, Sun, Mars, Jupiter etc.

In Dwadashottari, Panchottari, Shashtabdika, Chaturasiti Sama, Dwisaptati Sama and Shattrimsatisama Dasas, the conditions under which they apply are totally different. The divisors, in order to determine the Dasa running at birth, under the above systems are 8, 7, 7, 7, 8 and 8 respectively, which drastically alter the Nakshatra rulership pattern. In Shashtihayani Dasa system, as in Ashtottari, the Nakshatras are grouped into clusters but of 3 and 4 respectively and come under the Dasas of Jupiter, Sun, Mars, Moon, Mercury, Venus, Saturn and Rahu. The duration of the Dasas here is quite arbitrary, the first 3 Dasas are each of 10 years and the last five, each of 6 years.

So long as the divisor is 9, the Nakshatra rulerships apply in their natural order in the Zodiac and this is possible only in Vimshottari Dasa as the Zodiac comprises of 3 cycles of the same rulers. But once the divisor changes as seen above, the Nakshatra rulerships in the Bhachakra are thrown out of gear. This is an important point to be noted when experimenting with different Dasa systems and which can drastically affect the line of interpretation.

There are other Dasas like Lagnadi Rasi Dasa, Kala, Chakra, Kalachakra, Chara, Trikona, Sthira, Karaka, Brahmagraha, Drig Dasas, all based on different factors and determinants such as the birth occurring at night or day or in different Horas or if the Sun is in the Ascendant or if birth is in Krishna or Sukla Paksha etc., Rahu in Lagna or a Kendra or Trikona and other differing planetary factors. With so many Dasas to choose from yet it is only Vimshottari Dasa that Parasara emphasises more than once in **Hora** as being the best and the others as not acceptable.

अन्यास्तारादशाद्याश्य न सर्वा: सर्वसम्मता :
— Chap. 48-1

All are not acceptable by common consensus.

Kalachakra Dasa is also given great importance and in recent years, it has been projected as a necessary method to time events. But, of course, this may not be acceptable because **Kalachakra Dasa becomes relevant only in calculating longevity under specific conditions.** In fact, after calculating the Shadbalas of all planets and the Lagna, the strongest of these will determine which system of Dasa is to be followed for Ayurdaya.

If the strongest is Lagna — Amsa Ayurdaya ; if the Sun — Pinda Ayurdaya ; if the Moon — Naisargika Ayurdaya ; if Mars—Sataswaramsa Ayurdaya ; if Mercury — Nakshatra ; if Jupiter — Navamsa ; if Venus — Swaramsa and if Saturn, it has to be Karadaya Dasa.

But according to **Jataka Parijata,** when Venus is strongest in Shadbala, Kalachakra is to be applied.

According to **Phala Deepika,**

कालचक्रदशा ज्ञेया चन्द्रांशेशे बलान्विते ।

that is,

> *If the lord of the Navamsa occupied by the Moon is strongest in Shadbala, then only Kalachakra Dasa is to be applied.*

Yogini Dasa is also another Dasa system that is sometimes projected as leading to highly accurate results. In fact, it is said to be popular in certain parts of North India. Of course, every Dasa that Parasara defines has to be potent and capable of providing an unique angle to interpretation. But trying to understand even one single Dasa in all its completeness and ramifications may take more than a life time. However, from an academic angle one can always try to understand and experiment with the different Dasas. *(03-2000)*

Chapter 13

The Fallacy of Combining Different Dasa Systems

THERE IS A feeling amongst certain sections of astrological thought, that the best results can be obtained by combining different Dasa systems. For this, a chart is first analysed using the Vimshottari Dasa system and then, the conclusion is sought to be confirmed using some other Dasa system. For example, Ashtottari or Yogini Dasa system is applied to the same chart and if the interpretation concurs under both systems, it is taken as final. Such an approach is open to in-built contradictions.

An important factor overlooked in such experimentation is that some of the Dasas are applicable only under certain conditions, and therefore, cannot be applied to the chart under examination, unless it satisfies these conditions. For Yogini, however, no conditions are given, which may be taken to imply, it can be generally applied. But a careful examination of this Dasa system will reveal its deficiencies.

The Yogini Dasa system works in cycles of 36 years. One may see one cycle (Alpayu) or two cycles (Madhyayu — 2 x 36) or even three cycles as in Poornayu (3 x 36), in one's life time. That means the same Dasas can repeat not just two times but even 3 times in one's life-time.

But the interpretation becomes confusing as the same Dasas repeating at different stages and periods in life will have to be analysed and understood appropriately and this can lead to much confusion. For example, if a particular Yogini Dasa shows marriage at 25 years, the same Dasa repeating at 25 *plus* 36 years or 61 years should, again, show marriage. Such conclusions have to be carefully examined and contradictions reconciled. In Vimshottari, on the other hand, the same Dasa cannot occur more than once in one's life-time and therefore, the results it can grant are unique to that particular Dasa.

Yogini Dasa comes under 8 heads. It is also a Nakshatra Dasa, based on the Nakshatra occupied by the Moon at birth, but not directly but in a round-about manner depending upon the exact longitude of the Moon.

The Nakshatras, Aswini onwards, are given sequential numbers 1 to 27, *i.e.*, Aswini - 1, Bharani-2, Krittika - 3 etc.

There are 8 Dasas in Yogini — Mangala, Pingala, Dhanya, Bhramari, Bhadrika, Ulka, Siddha and Sankata identified with the Moon, Sun, Jupiter, Mars, Mercury, Saturn, Venus and Rahu respectively.

The digit 3 is added to the sequential number of the birth-Nakshatra and the sum is divided by 8. The remainder

Order	Yogini	Ruler	Duration
1	Mangala	Moon	1
2	Pingala	Sun	2
3	Dhanya	Jupiter	3
4	Bhramari	Mars	4
5	Bhadrika	Mercury	5
6	Ulka	Saturn	6
7	Siddha	Venus	7
8	Sankata	Rahu	8

The Fallacy of Combining Different Dasa Systems | 159

shows the Yogini Dasa running at birth with Mangala being the first of the series. The Dasa periods starting with Mangala are of 1, 2, 3, 4, 5, 6, 7 and 8 years duration respectively as shown in the Table.

The balance of Dasa at birth is determined by the rule of three.

Chart 41 : Born 24-10-1949 at 3-33 p.m. (IST) at 13 N, 77E35 with a balance of 3 years, 3 month 18 days of Saturn Dasa at birth.

RAHU							ASCDT. MARS
ASCDT	Chart 41 Rasi			VENUS RAHU	Navamsa		MERC
JUPT			MARS SAT.	JUPT			KETU
	VENUS MOON	SUN	MERC. KETU		SUN	SAT. MOON	

Let us suppose the Janma Nakshatra or birth star is Anuradha (Chart 41). Counting from Aswini as 1, Anuradha is 17.

Add 3 to it. Divide the sum by 8. The quotient is set aside. The remainder represents the Yogini Dasa operative at birth.

$$17+3 = \frac{20}{8} = = 2 \; Quotient + 4 \; Remainder$$

The *remainder 4* shows the Dasa running at birth as Bhramari ruled by Mars.

Moon = 14^0 20' (Anuradha - 4).

That is, 2^0 20' (= 140') of Anuradha is yet to be traversed.

The Dasa at birth is of Bhramari.
Therefore,
$13^0\ 20'\ :\ 4 \times 12\ :\ :\ $ Arc in Anuradha remaining to be traversed $:\ x$

$$x = \frac{4 \times 12 \times 140}{800} = 8\cdot 4 \text{ months}$$

Balance of Bhramari = 8 months 12 days.

Now in Vimshottari, for Anuradha $14^0\ 20'$, the Dasa would be of Saturn which means the native would experience Saturn Dasa for 3 years 3 months 3 days (approximately) after birth and then of Mercury, for 17 years. The positions of planets in the natal chart would determine the results in this case.

If we go by Yogini Dasa, the Dasa of Bhramari for 8 months 12 days and coming under Mars will be controlled by the position of Mars at birth. Then, it would be Bhadrika Dasa coming under Mercury and running for 5 years. After that, it would be Ulka or the period ruled by Saturn and this will be for 6 years. Results under Yogini will be controlled by Mercury's position for the period from the 2nd year to the 7th year, approximately; the 8th year onwards it will be ruled by Saturn. Therefore, the position of Mercury and Saturn in the birth-chart will control the events in the native's life upto 14 years, the first year coming under Mars. But according to Vimshottari, after 3 years of Saturn, the effect of Mercury will be experienced till the native's 20th year. Now, to apply these details to chart interpretation.

One of the simplest clues to get the feel of a chart is given in **Jataka Parijata** (Chap. XVIII-17).

करोति यद्भावगत: स्वपाके तद्भावजन्यं त्वशुभं शुभं वा ।
शुभं शुभव्योमचरस्य पाके पापस्य दाये त्वशुभं वदन्ति ॥
— J.P. XVIII-17

meaning,

A planet produces its effect upon the Bhava it occupies during its Dasa, this effect being good or bad according to the nature of the planet. If the planet be a benefic one, good is to be expected, during its Dasa, to the Bhava concerned; if the planet is malefic the Bhava will suffer evil.

यद्धातुखेटस्य दशापहारे तद्धातुवित्तायतिमहुरार्या:।
धातुक्षयं पापवियच्चरस्य पाकेऽभिवृद्धि शुभदस्य धातो: ॥
— J.P. XVIII-19

Likewise,

Whatever metal or article is assigned to a planet, the acquisition of property in that metal or article takes place during its Dasa or Bhukti. If the planet is malefic, there is a diminishing of that metal or article in that Dasa.

सपत्नखेटोपगतस्य पाके सपत्नवृद्धिसकलार्थनाशनम् ।
यत्कर्मकर्तृग्रहपाककाले तत्कर्मसिद्धि प्रवदन्तिसन्त: ॥
— J.P. XVIII 20

During the Dasa of a planet associated with a hostile one, enemies will multiply and all undertakings will fail. Of whatever business or concern, a planet is a Karaka (promoter), that concern will succeed, as the wise say, during the Dasa of the planet.

In the example case of Anuradha Nakshatra, under Vimshottari and Yogini, the Dasas would be as follows :

Vimshottari Dasas

Saturn	-	3 years
Mercury	-	17 years
Ketu	-	7 years
		27 Years

Yogini Dasas

Bhramari(Mars)	-	0 year 8 months 12 days
Bhadrika (Mercury)	-	5 years
Ulka(Saturn)	-	6 years
Siddha (Venus)	-	7 years
Sankata (Rahu)	-	8 years
		26 Years

The native, both during school and college, obtained distinction in educational life. Lots of books were also available to the native with access to good libraries and collection of rare books on different subjects. Schooling began in the 3rd year just as Mercury Dasa began. Education continued right through and into the first 15 months of Ketu Dasa. The Vimshottari Dasa of Mercury explains these results very well, as Mercury, as 5th and 8th lord is exalted in the 8th in the natal chart.

But according to Yogini, after about 8 months of Bhramari Mars, the next 5 years are assigned to Bhadrika Mercury. During this period, education was indeed good. Then it was Saturn's Ulka Dasa for the next 6 years, when also, educational pursuits fared well. But the results had nothing to do with Saturn or his position in the 7th with 10th lord Mars. Nor was there any drudgery and physical overwork that is associated with Saturn. Nor were the activities in any way connected with Mars or his 10th lordship. And both Mars and Saturn have little do with academics. From the 12th year to the 19th, it was Siddha Dasa coming under Venus placed in the 10th house with Neechabhanga Vargottama Moon. The results had nothing to do directly with Venus or his 10th house position or his 4th and 9th lordship, although, the native's academic success was marked by distinction and which can, indirectly, be attributed to the 10th house Venus. Rahu's Sankata Dasa after that gave distinction but brought studies to a halt. As the occupant of the 2nd house, Rahu should not have come in the way of continuing education. Most of the results were distinctly related to Mercury, his 5th house lordship, his Karakattwa and his position of exaltation which fit in with the Vimshottari Dasa of Mercury and then of Ketu, with Ketu occupying a sign ruled by Mercury, and therefore, capable of reflecting the results of an exalted Mercury.

Yogini Dasa lords cannot explain the results as clearly as the Vimshottari Dasa lords. Of course, one swallow does not make a summer. Nevertheless, this and several other cases have shown the greater accuracy of Vimshottari Dasa over other Dasa systems in our humble experience. This is an area that carries great potential for experimentation and research. Applying different Dasa systems to the same chart can help to unravel their scope as well as limitations in comparision to Vimshottari Dasa.

(05-2000)

Chapter 14

Muhurtha, Prasna and Political Predictions

Chapter 14

Mahurkha, Prison, and
Hoffman Predictions

A MUHURTHA, for a political occasion, is chosen astrologically to ensure the government sworn-in then completes its term. That is one way of looking at the Muhurtha. Many times, its interpretation along the lines of a birth chart gives satisfactory results. If the birth chart heralds the advent of its native into this world, the Muhurtha chart marks the beginning of a venture or project in an individual life or in the national context. So, the swearing-in chart of a government can be used to find clues to the fate of the government in question.

The green signal to read a Prasna chart as a birth chart has the sanction of classical authorities (**Prasna Tantra, Prasna Marga**) and when experience supports the use of a Muhurtha chart as a birth chart (in the context of the projects for which the Muhurtha is calculated), we can experiment trying to interpret a Muhurtha chart as a Prasna chart. The demarcation between the two dims and a sensitive interpretation can arrive at good results. But let us always bear in mind the roles of the two are not identical although each can be used in the place of the other in certain circumstances. The launching of a project, especially of political significance, is almost always accompanied by hope on one side and by apprehensions on the other of how long it will endure and how it will fare. While these questions are there alright when a Muhurtha is being adhered to, that they are not directed at the astrologer is what comes in the way of qualifying a Muhurtha as a full-fledged Prasna. Nevertheless, it has overtones of a Prasna and can give as much of a clue as a regular question directed at the astrologer when the Muhurtha becomes a *defacto* Prasna chart.

Treating the chart for the swearing-in time of Rajiv Gandhi as a Prasna, the picture becomes clear (Chart 42).

Chart 42 : Rajiv Gandhi sworn-in as prime minister on 31-12-1984 at 5-29 p.m. (IST) at 28N39, 77E13.

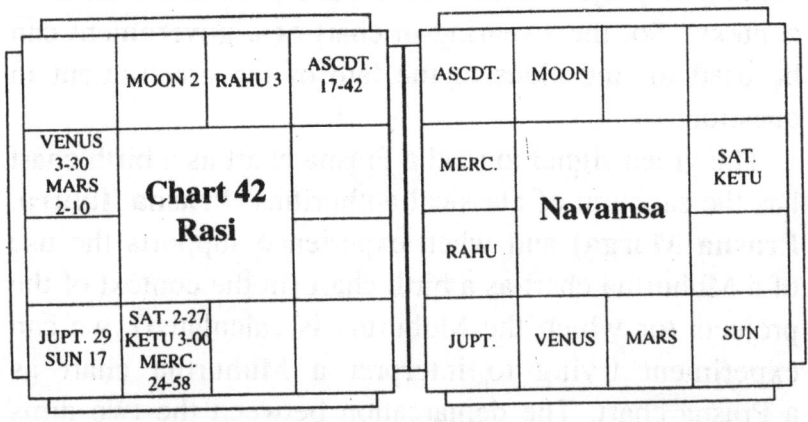

The Ascendant in Chart 1 is aspected by a benefic and its significator (as 10th lord) Jupiter indicating the government would work its term out. The Sun's aspect as Karaka is also significant.

In India, the practice of the astrologer being one of the important counsellors of the king can be traced to very distant times. During the period of the Cholas and other monarchs, the court astrologer was a very important personage. The King had to have 5 assemblies — one each of people, priests, astrologers, physicians and ministers — to guide him in the administration.

No expedition or war was begun without recourse to astrological guidance. Deposed kings bided their time to correspond with favorable planetary positions (especially the transits of Saturn) to set out on war to regain their lost kingdoms. Even in the **Ramayana** period, we have Vasishta guiding Dasaratha. Dasaratha is worried when Mars, Sun and Rahu conjoin on his Nakshatra and fears a great calamity will befall the kingdom. In the **Mahabharata,** Duryodhana approaches Sahadeva for the best Muhurta to start the war so as to win it.

During the Second World War, many important decisions such as troop movements were timed in accordance with astrological advice. The role of an astrologer in running the country was recognised as of great importance.

Brihat Samhita II – 26

अप्रदीपा यथा रात्रिरनादित्यं यथा नभः ।
तथाऽसावंत्सरो राजा भ्रमत्यन्ध इवाध्वनि ॥

Just as the night devoid of lights or lamps is utterly blind, and the sky without the Sun dark even so will a king grope in life in the dark like a blind man on the way, if he is not guided by a good astrologer.

The late Prof. B. Suryanarain Rao who pioneered astrological journalism in India and who brought astrology to the English-knowing public of India, had a number of remarkable correct predictions to his credit. Analysing the chart for the commencement of the lunar year Ananda

(1914-15), he observed thus in the March 1916 issue of THE ASTROLOGICAL MAGAZINE.

> *There will be sudden outbreaks of passion and excitement among the armies leading to anarchy and denunciation of old kingly authority, great loss and consternation and the war fever will be at its highest pitch. A European war is threatened .... and the United States should be very careful in not being dragged into a ruinous war. Two deaths among the European royalties are indicated and one of them will be from violence of treachery. Political relations all over the world during the months of August and September will be highly excited on account of the solar and lunar eclipses following one after the other within a fortnight.*

The assassination of the Arch Duke of Austria and the outbreak of the First World War are all matters of history and need no exposition.

DR. RAMAN has identified a 20-year periodicity in the correlation between the deaths of American Presidents in office and Jupiter-Saturn conjunctions. Whenever a US President has been elected under a Jupiter-Saturn conjunction, he has died in office — sometimes due to violence and sometimes, a natural death. But the important point is, he has died without completing his term.

1840 – W.H. Harrison, elected President, died in office from an assassin's bullet.

1960 – Abraham Lincoln, elected President, was assassinated.

1880 – James A. Gerfield, elected President, was shot dead.
1900 – William Mackinley, elected President for a second term and died later during his term of office.
1920 – Warren C. Harding, elected President and died in the White House.
1940 – Franklin Roosevelt, elected President to a third term and died in office.
1960 – Kennedy elected President and was shot dead in office.
1980 – Reagan was elected President, but escaped assassination attempts, thanks to astrology.

Very few people know that astrological ideas and advice shaped administrative policy of the United States between 1980 and 1988 when Reagan was President. Through Nancy, wife of President Reagan, Joan, a California-based astrologer, had a direct line to the President and the work she did, affected the top level of Government in the USA.

All press conferences, most speeches, the State of the Union addresses, the take-offs and landings of Air Force One (military aircraft meant for Reagan), the time of Ronald Reagan's debate with Carter and the two debates with Walter Mandela; all extended trips abroad as well as the shorter trips and one-day excursions, the announcement that Reagan would run for a second term, briefings for almost all the summits except Moscow, the time to begin the Moscow trips, congressional arm-twisting, the second Inaugural Oath of Office, the announcement of Anthony

Kennedy's Supreme Court nomination, President Reagan's first operation for cancer and the time for Nancy's masectomy etc., were all based on astrological factors chosen by Joan.

The President was exposed as little as was possible to the public and the media during astrologically sensitive periods to protect him from both the physical and political dangers that were indicated in his chart. Summit meetings between the Super-powers, changing Ronald Reagan's "Evil Empire" attitude, so that he went to Geneva prepared to meet a different kind of Russian leader and one he could convince of doing things the US way were all based on astrological advice.

During this seven-year period, the President's horoscope was analysed sometimes on an hour-to-hour basis both for political reasons as well as for safety. In fact, Ronald Reagan was the first President elected in a zero year to survive his term of office since John F. Kennedy who was assassinated while in office in 1960.

In **Prasna Tantra** and other works on horary astrology, there is always a section devoted to questions on winning or losing kingdoms and related matters. These combinations can be applied to winning elections or the fall of government.

In questions bearing on the acquisition of a kingdom, the Lagna is said to represent the efforts of the querent, the 7th is said to rule the help and support he has, the 10th, the benefits of gaining the kingdom, and the 4th, help from friends. As in the natal chart, the 3rd rules colleagues and subordinates, the 2nd rules finance, and the 6th, enemies and these Bhavas and the positions of their rulers show the respective influences those factors have in the mission of obtaining a kingdom. A weak Lagna or Lagna lord afflicted can mean destruction of the kingdom.

One of the most effective clues for whether a government will last full term or not can be had in Slokas 120 and 121 of **Prasna Tantra.** This text is said to be by one Neelakanta Daivagnya and has been translated into English by DR. B.V.RAMAN.

The query "whether or not the king holds the country permanently" should be answered thus : *If out of the lords of* the Ascendant and the 10th, the slower-moving lord is in *a quadrant, the authority will be permanent.* Otherwise, the sway will be temporary.

If the slower-moving planet is retrograde and occupies the 4th house and there is Kamboola Yoga, the kingdom will slip out of the king's rule for some time but he gets it back quickly. If there is Musaripha, the chances of getting back the kingdom are bleak.

These combinations can be adapted to interpret political fortunes in a democracy also.

The same rule can be applied to the chart concerning Rajiv Gandhi. The Ascendant is Gemini and its ruler is Mercury. The 10th lord is Jupiter and he, the slower planet of the two, is placed in a Kendra in the 7th house. Rajiv Gandhi's rule was permanent. In today's parlance, he did complete his term of office.

The second Sloka requires that the slower planet be retrograde and in the 4th house in a Kamboola Yoga in which case, the lost kingdom will be regained.

Chart 43 : N. T. Rama Rao sworn-in as chief minister on 12-12-1914 at 12-01 p.m. at 17N26, 78E27.

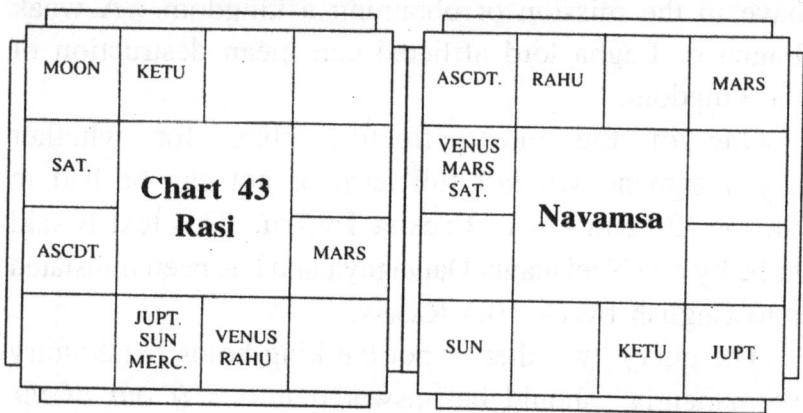

Taking note of the Lagna lord Saturn and 10th lord Venus (Chart 43), we find Venus who is the faster of the two is in a Kendra. NTR did not complete his term; he was deposed in a family coup master-minded by his sons-in-law. Additionally, we may note Lagna lord Saturn is afflicted by malefics Mars and the 10th lord by Rahu. Mars as 11th lord is the 7th lord from the 5th and afflicts

Chart 44 : Question Time : 25-3-1995 at 4-30 p.m. at 13N, 77E35.

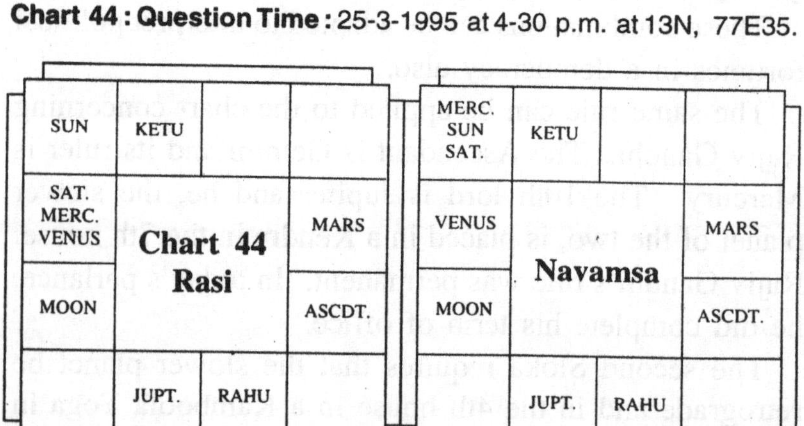

the Muhurtha Lagna. The role of the sons-in-law in bringing down NTR is only too well-known.

We come to a most interesting chart (Chart 44) pertaining to the question when Deve Gowda was the chief minister of Karnataka, if he would complete his term of office. He was sworn-in on 11-12-1994 at 6-30 p.m. The question came on 25-3-1995 at 4-30 p.m. at Bangalore.

The Ascendant in Chart 44 is aspected by both benefics and malefics. But if you take up the Bhava chart, the Ascendant is aspected by Venus. But Venus is a natural benefic, yet, he failed to let Deve Gowda complete his full term. Venus here is the 10th lord. Between the Lagna and the 10th lord, that is, the Sun and Venus, Venus is the faster planet. Venus in a Kendra, therefore, does not show full term. All the same, as a benefic, Venus, aspecting the Ascendant had its favorable influence. Deve Gowda relinquished his chief ministership but only to occupy the more powerful office of the prime minister.

Another combination that can be equally applied to political predictions is also from **Prasna Tantra** Sloka 113 which means,

There will be no success or realisation of the object if the lord of the sign occupied by the lord of the Ascendant is in unfavorable houses. Immense difficulties have to be faced if the Ascendant lord is combust. If there is a square, there will be strife and quarrels.

The Sloka and the combination can be suitably adapted to questions on the longevity of an elected government also. Success, in this context, can be interpreted as continuing power during the full term of its statutory life.

Chart 45 : Chandrasekhar sworn-in as prime minister on 10-11-1990 at 11-00 a.m. (IST) at 28N39, 77E13.

```
Chart 45 Rasi:
- MARS (R) 19-14
- KETU 9.35, JUPT. 20-38
- MOON 3-43
- SUN 25-17, VENUS 27-27
- MERC. 6-33
- SAT. 28-16, ASCDT. 22-12
- RAHU 9-35

Navamsa:
- RAHU
- MOON, SUN
- MARS (R), VENUS
- MERC.
- KETU
- ASCDT.
- SAT.
- JUPT.
```

Chart 45 cast for the time when Chandrasekhar was sworn in as prime minister can also be treated as a Prasna chart.

Jupiter as the Ascendant lord is in the 8th with Ketu. Its ruler Moon is in the 9th aspected by malefic Mars (R). The Ascendant is not vacant but has an occupant Saturn in it. So that we will have to consider this sign as more important than that occupied by the Ascendant lord. So, we see where Saturn's sign-dispositer Jupiter is. Jupiter is in the 8th, an unfavorable house. That means there will be no success. In other words, the Government under Chandrasekhar would not complete its full term.

We can analyse the same chart more simply applying the fundamental rules of horary astrology and arrive at the same conclusion.

The Ascendant Sagittarius has a malefic Saturn in it aspected by the retrograde Mars from the 6th house. The Ascendant lord Jupiter does not aspect the Ascendant or the 10th house. No other benefic does so. Saturn as a malefic aspects the 10th house. Thus, there are only malefic influences acting on the chart which cannot let the Government work for long.

The 10th lord Mercury is in the 12th aspected by Mars (retrograde) and caught between malefics, Sun and Saturn. If ever there was a Government whose working at every single step was obstructed, Chandrasekhar's would easily qualify as the best choice for this unique discount. Not a day passed when the Congress (I) on whose support the Government hung for dear life did not bully it and do everything possible to scuttle its proper functioning. The 7th lord Mercury in the 12th (the house of loss) led to the collapse of the Government (Mercury as 10th lord) when the Congress (I) crossed all norms of democratic decency threatening to withdraw its support. *(1990's)*

Chapter 15

Planets and Underground Water Sources

SUMMER IN full force in most of India — cities, town, villages — means water shortages and scarcity assume menacing proportions. This scarcity is not natural. It is man-made. Poor planning and corruption that percolates into every single rung of the bureaucracy are the factors behind this acute shortage of a vital element. Bore-wells have been dug indiscriminately in urban areas and so poorly planned that many of them have simply dried up after an initial gush of water.

Population growth at an alarming rate is also, to some extent, responsible for many of the ills we face today. Planning has been haphazard. The glamorous has been pampered at the cost of the practical with the result problems beseech the comman man at every level of existence. Space science and technology are projected as the panacea for all our ills and concentrating on them and on our image in the international space-club has done little to provide the commoner with the basic needs of food, shelter and clothing. What is worse, if food is not available that is bad enough but even water, the vital element, is hard to come by. In the cities, people who can afford, and they form a miniscule fraction of the population, buy water in tankers paying sizeable sums per tanker. But what about the rest ? The Governments in the past were busy with *utsavs* and festivals and *melas* abroad, elections, setting up and toppling governments, misappropriating crores of rupees and such other exciting activity, the fact the common man was a human being with vital, if not basic needs, was all but forgotten.

Space science peers even claimed to be exploring the possibility of harnessing water with the help of satellites. Yet, other science peers opined that drinking water problems could be improved by redesigning storm water drains. While these grandiose ideas and plans were being discussed and reviewed, countless summers sped by making the problem that much more acute each year. Modern space techniques are expensive but of little use, that is, constructive use. Their destructive potential indeed, tremendous as has beeen amply demonstrated in the wars in Europe which saw highly sophisticated sensors and imageries being employed.

Astrology, not orthodox science and even less, space science and satellites, can provide the answer to the acute water problems in our country.

Varahamihira in his famous *nagnum opus*, the **Brihat Samhita**, has dealt exhaustively with the means and methods of identifying underground water sources. The chapter *Dakargalam* meaning "divining *udaka* or water" details out a systematic and comprehensive methodology based on different kinds of natural factors to locate subterranean springs. Modern techniques of hydrologic exploration, especially the satellite sensing variety, are painfully complicated, expensive and rarely successful. Effective costs is one of the weighty reasons next only to the success rate or lack of it by these methods that pleads for exploring the simple but highly workable methods offered by astrology. It is not for nothing that this science is known as **Jyotisha**, the science that radiates light wherever there is darkness and ignorance. The methods, outlined by Varahamihira closely examined without bias, show a link between all the phenomena involved in hydrologic exploration confirming the theory of cause and effect being present in the environment which is another dimension of the basic postulate of Jyotisha or astrology.

Ancient Western literature on hydrology, primarily Greek, in contrast to Jyotisha, is unreliable and full of wild theories on the origin of ground water.

The **Bible** says the sea is the source of all springs. The bottom of the sea, according to it, is said to have hole through which water escapes, flows through subterranean channels and emerges as a spring.

Thales, the Ionian philosopher, says all water comes from the oceans. The winds push the sea water through rock and lift them up through the mountains to emerge as springs.

Plato, the great philosopher, was even more phantasical in his explanation of underground sources. He said there was a huge underground cavern called *tartarus* filled with water from which all the water sources got their water. These waters, he said, returned to the cavern through sub-surface passages.

Senoca, the founder of the Stoic Philosophy, refused to accept that rainfall could be the source of springs as rainwater could penetrate only a few feet into the earth while the springs came from deep down. And all these thinkers were of comparatively recent origin belonging to the post-600 or 650 B.C. period.

In the **Vedas** however, dating far far back, there are valuable references to underground water. In more recent times, **Varahamihira**, in his treatise, says he has only collected information and facts already known and expounded by Rishis, and does not claim to be their originator. He assertively says almost all underground water is derived from rain by infiltration from the surface. Listing different surface phenomena drawn from both *flora* and *fauna*, Varahamihira even gives the exact location of the underground water and the depth at which it can be found.

The unit of distance employed is the *Purusha*. *Purusha* is the height of a man and is defined as the distance (height) covered by an average man standing with his hands outstretched overhead, this being roughly equivalent to 7·5 feet or 90 inches. One *Purusha* is equal to 5 *Hastas* which makes one *Hasta* equal to 1·5 feet or 18 inches.

Unlike the complicated techniques of modern science, Varahamihira's are outright simple. He says, to begin with, indications for water by trees in forest tracts may not work in desert regions.

जम्ब्वाश्वोदग्धस्तैस्त्रिभि: शिराधो नरद्वये पूर्वा
मृल्लोहगन्धिका पाण्डुरा च पुरुषेऽत्र मण्डूक: ॥

— LIV – 8

A *Jambu* (a rose-apple) tree occurring in a dry region (but in areas of vegetation) means an easterly vein at a depth of 2 *Purushas* (15 feet) and at a distance of 3 *Hastas* (18 x 3 = 54 inches) or 4·5 feet to its North. Confirmatory clues are the soil has an iron-like smell at a depth of a *Purusha* (7·5 feet), next, pale white clay, and then a frog in that order are likely to be pitched on.

A termite mound near a Jambu tree to its East shows plenty of sweet water yielding for a long time (दीर्घं कालं बहु तोयं). The water will be at 3 *Hastas* (54 inches = 4·5 feet) to the South of the tree and at a depth of 2 *Purushas* (15 feet). A fish at a depth of half a *Purusha* (45 inches), then a dove coloured rock, and then blue clay confirm water after the digging is begun. The presence of fish may imply a locked bowl of water underneath the ground.

In a similar manner, Varaha refers to various factors involving trees and termite mounds or anthills (वल्मीक) and confirmatory factors such as non-poisonous snakes, black frogs, rats, turtles, clay or rock of different hues etc., as showing water. General clues include the presence of a frog at the foot of a tree, grassy patch in a grassless place, thorny shrub in the midst of non-thorny trees, a white or low-lying branch and date palms with two crowns. In all, he lists about 32 distinct types of plants and trees accompanied by several other pointers as showing ground water.

Varahamihira also tells us where to look for and find water in desert regions (मरुदेशे). If clues indicated for forest regions are present in desert areas, then the digging has to go deeper down two-fold. In certain spots, water can be found beneath a rock and he outlines how the rocks can be blasted. Rocks answering certain descriptions are said to be perennial sources of water and Varahamihira asserts such areas will never suffer drought (. . . . तेषामवृष्टिं भवते कदाचित् ।).

Water location is followed by details on construction of ponds, wells and tanks. He prescribes a mixture of antimony, myrobalan and other natural ingredients as an effective water-purifying agent to be used when the water is **blackish,** muddy, saltish, bitter, bereft of good taste or of **bad odour.**

Rohini, Pushya, Makha, the 3 Uttaras — Uttaraphalguni, **Uttarashada,** Uttarabhadrapada — Hasta, Anuradha, Dhanishta and Satabhisha are said to be favorable asterisms for sinking wells.

Varamihira's treatment is an integrated study of water ecology and shows the advanced scientific strides made in ancient India. The treatment of the subject shows the profound understanding the seers had of the inter-relation between living organisms and their environment extending to the cosmos as a whole.

While Varahamihira's methods are based on ecological factors, Kupa Prasna or horary astrology can also be equally applied to ascertaining if there is underground water in a particular stretch of land or premises.

Watery planets in watery signs at question time show copious water sources underground. The Moon and Venus are watery planets. Cancer, Scorpio and Pisces are the watery signs.

Watery planets in non-watery signs indicate very little water. Non-watery planets in non-watery signs show dry waterless depths.

Favorable influences on the Ascendant and the 4th house also signify water.

1. A moveable sign (Aries, Cancer, Libra or Capricorn) rising with Rahu and the Moon in it shows the presence of water.

2. The Sun in the 10th and Jupiter in the 4th is also indicative of water.

3. When the Moon is in the Ascendant and a malefic occupies the 4th, then also underground water is indicated.

4. If Capricorn rises with the Moon in the 7th, Venus in the 10th and Jupiter in Pisces, water is present.

5. If Venus and the Moon are exalted and aspected by debilitated planets, water is shown.

Some combinations with reference to Arudha are also given :

1. If Arudha is Virgo and the Moon is in Pisces aspected by Jupiter and Venus, water will be found.

2. If Arudha in Virgo is hemmed between the Moon and Venus, then also it shows water.

3. When a fixed sign rising on the Lagna is occupied by Venus and Saturn or the Moon is in Leo with the Arudha falling in a watery sign, it shows water.

4. If Arudha is Taurus occupied by the Moon, it shows a water source underground.

5. If Pisces is Arudha, the Moon is in Virgo and Jupiter occupies Gemini, water is shown.

When these combinations are present, it is safe to presume there is underground water in the premises and digging a well would be successful.

The next step would be to try to locate the exact spot where water is available. The *Chandra Gupti Chakra* offers guidance at this point.

It is a diagrams of the area of the premises divided into 28 rectangular segments, any one or more of which may carry water underground.

This diagram has to be drawn according to particular rules depending upon the time of question.

If the question is asked between morning and noon, the astrologer should face the East; if between noon and sunset, South; if between sunset and midnight, West; and he should face the North if the question is asked between midnight and the following sunrise.

Suppose **ABCD** is the area in which one is looking for underground water. The dimensions of this piece of land are $l \times b$. The arrow **N** shows North. If the question, for example, is put between noon and sunset, the person should face South when constructing the *Chandra Gupti*

A   O   B

↑N

1	2	3	4	5	16	17
28	9	8	7	6	15	18
27	10	11	12	13	14	19
28	25	24	23	22	21	20

l

D b C

Chakra. He should place the plan of the area in such a way he occupies **0** with reference to the side **AB** and proceed to construct the diagram as follows :

Eight equidistant lines are drawn longitudinally between **A** and **B** starting with **AD** and ending with **BC**, both inclusive. Next 5 equidistant lines are drawn across horizontally including **AB** and **DC**. These lines divide the site-area into 28 distinct rectangular blocks which are numbered in a particular way. Starting with the block corresponding to the corner **A**, enter the numbers 1 to 5 horizontally. Enter 6 below 5. Then enter 7, 8, 9 horizontally towards the left. Place 10 under 9 and mark 11, 12, 13, 14 towards the right. Mark 15 above 14 and 16, above 15. Place 17 to the right of 16 and the rest of the numbers upto 28 in sequential order in the remaining blocks moving downwards from 17.

Method One : These 28 blocks are assigned 28 equal parts of the day's length. That is, duration of day (60 Ghatis) is divided equally into 28 units. Each works out to 2·142 Ghatis.

Next, go back to the question time. Determine the number of Ghatis of the question time from sunrise. Divide this by 2·142 and we get *Dinarsha* counted from Aswini.

The Nakshatra occupied by the rising sign at the time of question is the Udaya Nakshatra.

After determining the Dinarsha, place it in the 1st block at **A**. Count according to the order marked in the figure till you reach Udaya Nakshatra. Count again from Udaya Nakshatra in the order marked in the figure to the Nakshatra occupied by the Moon at question time. The block occupied by this Nakshatra marks the spot in the site where underground water is present.

Method Two : Another school of writers gives a different method. Place Aswini in the block marked 1. From here, count to the asterism occupied by a watery planet in the Prasna chart. This also gives the spot where a well can be sunk.

Method Three : Place the Udaya Nakshatra in the

3rd square. From here, count upto the Nakshatra occupied by a watery planet. This also gives the location of water.

These methods work exceptionally well in practice.

In the example here (Chart 46), the querent wanted to find out if he could sink a well in his site.

According to **Uttarakalamrita**, digging of a well comes under the 4th house. The 4th house here is Cancer occupied by exalted 9th lord Jupiter and aspected by Saturn. Rahu-Ketu influence the 4th house in Vargottama strength. The 4th lord Moon is in the 9th in exchange of signs with 9th lord Jupiter, the former being Vargottama. This Parivartana Yoga involving the 4th and 9th (good fortune) houses with the lords being strongly placed is a highly favorable indication for finding water in the site.

Chart 46 : Question Time : 11-3-1991 at 10-15 a.m. (IST) at 13N, 77E35.

MERC. VENUS	ASCDT.	MARS	ARUDHA	VENUS	SAT.		SUN
SUN	Rasi Chart 46		JUPT. KETU		Navamsa		KETU
SAT. RAHU				JUPT. RAHU			MARS MERC.
MOON				ASCDT. MOON			

Saturn's aspect and Jupiter's debility in Navamsa indicate not a very rich or strong spring; nevertheless, a fairly good source is possible because of the strength of the two planets involved.

The next question was naturally to locate the spot where water could be found. A *Chandra Gupti Chakra* was drawn.

Time of question = 10-15 a.m. (IST)
Sunrise on date of question = 6-20 a.m. (IST)
Difference = 3h.46 m.= 226 minutes

Time of question after sunrise = 9·4166 Gh.

Dividing this by $2\frac{1}{7}$ or 2·142,

$$\text{we get } \frac{9·41166}{2·142} = 4·396$$

Therefore, the Dinarsha is the 5th from Aswini which makes it Mrigasira. Insert Mrigasira in the first square (*Figure 1*). The Udaya Nakshatra or the Nakshatra rising on the Eastern horizon at the time of the query is Krittika. So, we start from Mrigasira and count to the Udaya Nakshatra Krittika in the diagram. Mark it.

Dinarsha 1 Mrigasira	2	3	4	5	16 Uttarashada	17
28	9	8	7	6	15	18
27	10	11	12	13	14	19
Udaya Nakshatra 26 Krittika	25	24	23	22	21	20

Figure 1

The Moon at question time is in Uttarashada. So we count from Udaya Nakshatra Krittika to Uttarashada in the sequential order of the numbers marked. This spot (block 16 in *Figure 1*) holds water underground.

Since the house was already built and the space shown in *Figure 1* had a structure at this spot, the spot shown in *Figure 2* (Method 2) was chosen and a rig set up to bore a well here successfully.

The watery planets are the Moon and Venus. The Moon is in Uttarashada. Venus is in Revati. Let us take the Moon and count from Aswini to the constellation the Moon occupies, that is, Uttarashada in *Figure 2*. Venus is stronger being in a watery sign. So, the spot marked by Revati also shows water.

But in another case, a water spot was sought in a site of 50 ft. x 56 ft. dimension. While the *Chandra Gupti Chakri* shows the location, the Prasna must first be checked if at all there is any underground water in the site in question.

1 Aswini	2	3	4	5	16	17
28	9	8	7	6	15	18
27 Revati	10	11	12	13	14	19
26	25	24	23	22	21 Uttarashada	20

Figure 2

The Rasi chart is slightly misleading although the Bhava chart gives a very definite answer.

Chart 47 : Question Time : 20-4-1991 at 4-15 p.m. at 13N, 77E35.

MERC. SUN	VENUS	MOON MARS	
	Rasi Chart 47		JUPT. KETU
SAT. RAHU			
			LAGNA 4-36 ARUDHA

The Ascendant Virgo in Chart 47 is aspected by the Sun and Mars, both hot, dry, fiery planets. The 4th house is aspected by Mars and the 4th lord by Saturn. The Moon's aspect misses the 4th house in Bhava. This led to the conclusion there could be no underground water in that site. But the owner went by the geologist's assurance after the usual "scientifically conducted and approved tests there was, indeed, water and the bore-well rig could start running". Dutifully the owner began the boring operation. One hundred and ten feet below ground level, he had still not found any water. So, they drilled even more fiercely until they had reached 180 feet without success. The owner gave up in utter frustration after parting with a sizeable chunk of money for the drilling experiment. It is a pity private owners allow themselves to be misled by scientific jargon. It is even a greater pity that the space scientific satellites in our country claim to be able to locate underground water resources from the INSAT satellites deployed by the Space Department when most of the time they are unable to do it and the failures add up to prohibitive sums of money. Our ancient seers were not mere philosophers; they were scientists of the highest intellectual and moral calibre. Their findings, coming under the name of Jyotisha, are reliable and within the reach of the poorest of the poor. Just because their methods are so simple, they cannot be dismissed as superstition. Superstition today is the right word for the craze people have developed for the officially recognised sciences which promise a lot but deliver little. The awe, this reverential fear with which science is held and described as the panacea for all human ills and problems, is the biggest superstition of our times. An unbiased and diligent study of astrological factors in determining underground water sources will give tangible results and go a long way in meeting the acute shortage of this life-giving liquid faced by our people. (07-'91)

Chapter 16

Judging Ayurdaya — Some Broad Guidelines

THE BIRTH chart or horoscope is a map of the heavens at the time of birth and carries, for those who can decipher the planetary script, clues to the sequence of events that are littered between birth and death. The birth marks the descent of the soul on earth and its embodiment. Death means the shedding of the body. The soul undergoes a variety of experiences, some good and some bad and many, insignificant and trifling, between these two milestones of human existence. The chart which begins with the point of time a human life comes into existence also carries clues to when such existence ceases. A question perennially posed to the astrological savant, by those who have not been exposed to the proper and judicious application of astrology, is what purpose can be served by getting to know the span or length of life one is allotted. The next question that follows, and which is only a somewhat immature extension of the first is, can an astrological assessment show the exact time and date when death will overtake one.

The second question does not merit a serious answer. Nevertheless, let it not be understood that this implies there is no answer. The correct date and even time of death can be guaged but it is not an easy task and requires experienced skill and intuition to do it. But there is really no need to undertake such an exercise in most cases.

Exceptional circumstances of gravity may warrant it, however. Coming to the more interesting first question, any attempt to answer it in a complete and full sense would necessitate an exposition of the immense potential and wide range of application astrology has in planning one's life, time, finances, energy, resources, children and of course, relationships.

An understanding of longevity is of great help in making marital decisions. A short-lived marriage with one of the spouses dying prematurely can mark a traumatic period in life bringing in great dislocation at various levels, more so if there are small children. Major decisions like a change in the country of residence or heavy investments in securities or immoveable property can also benefit by a fore-knowledge of one's longevity. Even relatively minor decisions such as change in service from one employer to another or from the private sector to the public or *vice-versa* may be made more carefully with an eye on longevity.

One of the more crucial but little known areas of life where the longevity question becomes all important has to do with decisions related to major surgery. Though technological advances and breakthrough discoveries in surgical procedures and treatment have been making headlines, they are no guarantee of a patient's life and longevity. Not only that, with each new advance in the medical world, the financial burden on the patient only keeps mounting and raises the question of how reliable medical diagnosis and advice always are to warrant such drastic treatment with its accompanying costs which many can ill-afford. And more importantly, the question, which looms large in every case where a loved one is wheeled into the operation theatre, if such medical steps will save the patient can be handled more effectively when one has some clue to the approximate span of life the chart promises. Briefly put, the astrological estimate of longevity is an invaluable guide to making crucial and important decisions in life.

Let us begin with the simple case of the birth of a child in a family. Most urban families are increasingly tending to get nuclear and are made up of just the couple and the children. The trend is towards relatively few issues. Mostly two, but in some rare instances, may be three. Others are quite content with one child. This brings us to the question of family planning. Would it be advisable to avoid pregnancy again after the 1st or 2nd child ? That would seem a perfectly fair and ideal decision in the face of changing patterns in social thinking. But what would happen if, when irreversible measures for family planning have been taken recourse to to limit the family, and God forbid, the child or children die because of illness or an accident. Sometimes, children are kidnapped and even killed. No one can be sure such tragedies will not take place. And what happens when the only child which one dotes on disappears from one's life. This is where the question of longevity assumes great importance. There is no way one can be sure one's child will not be vulnerable to such cruel strokes of fate except through Jyotisha or astrology.

Every classical work, after dealing with the preliminary details of definitions and characteristics of planets, carries a detailed exposition of the subject of longevity or

Ayurdaya. Combinations for Balarishta or infant mortality (including childhood death) are listed first. Such combinations if carefully identified from the birth chart of the child can help young parents make a wise decision on whether to have another and when to limit the family. There are numerous Balarishta Yogas or combinations and the majority of them revolve round the Moon's position at birth. Balarishta Yogas limit life at the most to 8 years (अष्टौ बालारिष्टमादौ) but sometimes, to 12 years also.

The Moon in the Gandanta part of a Nakshatra, if aspected or conjoined with a malefic planet makes the child meet with early death. (The first quarter or Pada of Aswini, Makha and Moola and the last quarter or Pada of Aslesha, Jyeshta and Revati are known as Gandantas). The same result is also shown by the Moon occupying the मृत्यु (*Mrityu*) or fatal parts of different signs or if aspected by a malefic planet. The fatal points in each sign, according to **Jataka Parijata** (II-57), are 8^0 (Aries), 25^0 (Taurus), 22^0 (Gemini), 22^0 (Cancer), 21^0 (Leo), 1^0 (Virgo), 4^0 (Libra), 23^0 (Scorpio), 18^0 (Sagittarius), 20^0 (Capricorn), 20^0 (Aquarius) and 10^0 (Pisces).

Death in infancy or childhood is shown under the following conditions also :

(a) When the waning Moon occupies the rising sign and a malefic is in a Kendra or the 8th from Lagna.

(b) When benefics are in the 8th or 6th from the Lagna aspected by malefics.

(c) When Mars, Saturn, Sun are in conjunction in the 6th or 8th from Lagna with no benefic influences on them.

(d) When the Moon in the 1st, 6th, 8th or 12th is aspected by a malefic and there are no benefics in Kendras.

(e) When malefics are in the Lagna and the 7th and the Moon is with a malefic with no benefic aspect.

(f) When all the malefics are in the Lagna and the 8th, when no benefics occupy the Kendras and the Moon is in the 12th.

(g) When the Moon in conjunction with malefics occupies the Lagna, the 8th, 7th or 12th with no benefic aspects and there are no benefics in Kendras.

(h) When the Moon is in the 6th or the 8th aspected by malefics.

(i) When the Moon is with Rahu conjoined with Mars in the 8th house.

Chart 48 : Born 7-11-1975 at 7-30 p.m. at 13 N, 77 E 35 with a balance of 17 years 1 month 6 days of Venus Dasa at birth.

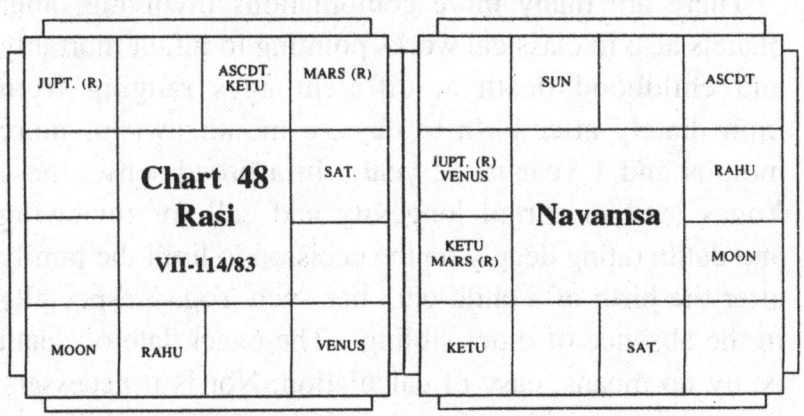

Chart 48 is of a boy who was kidnapped on 26-4-1983 when he was playing outside his house. The parents began to receive anonymous calls demanding a heavy ransom for the boy. The father of the boy agreed to pay the sum but wanted an assurance from the kidnappers, the child would be returned to him the same time the money changed hands. This, the kidnappers refused saying the money should reach them first; a day later, the boy would come. The parents grew suspicious and feared the worst. They asked to be allowed to talk to their child on the phone at least, but the kidnappers refused to oblige. After a few days, the calls stopped but the boy never returned home. He was murdered. The parents were never able to reconcile themselves to the tragic loss of their boy and went into a gloom that has now become an inseparable part of their lives, robbing them of all mental peace.

The Ascendant Taurus is occupied by Ketu. The Moon is in the 8th aspected by malefic Mars (R). There are no benefics in Kendras. These factors have produced a powerful Balarishta Yoga.

There are many more combinations involving other planets also in classical works pointing to infant mortality and childhood death at different ages ranging from immediately after birth to days, a month, two or more months and 1 year to 12 years. In a broad sense, these Yogas tend to curtail longevity and call for reviewing and deliberating deeply on the decision to limit the family after the birth of a child who has such Yogas, especially in the absence of older siblings. The exact date of death is, by no means, easy of calculation. Nor is it necessary to work it out either. But the clue to the possibility of a tragedy in childhood should help gear a couple plan its family better.

Briefly put, *an afflicted Moon, especially in the Dustanas (6th, 8th or 12th) with Rahu also there is a strong Balarishta factor, notwithstanding the presence of even Jupiter in the Ascendant.* — **Jataka Parijata** (IV-4)

विलग्नयातस्त्वपि देवमन्त्री विनाशरि:फारिगते शशाङ्के।
विलोकिते पापवियच्चरेण विभानुना मृत्युपैति बाला: ॥

Conversely, a powerfully placed Moon is a good augury for lonvevity.

चंद्र: संपूर्णगात्रस्तु सौम्यक्षेत्रांशगोपि वा ।
सर्वारिष्टनिहन्ता स्यात् विशेषच्छुभवीक्षित: ॥

The Moon with his digits full or in the house or Navamsa of a benefic planet becomes a destroyer of all evil; this, all the more so, when aspected by a benefic planet. (ibid IV-82)

In cases where Balarishta factors are present, the following tend to neutralise these adverse indications and extend longevity.

(a) When the Lagna lord is strong and aspected or conjoined with a benefic and is in a Kendra position without malefic aspects (जीवति दीर्घमायु:).

(b) When Jupiter, Venus or Mercury is in a Kendra in strength and free from malefic aspect or conjunction.

(c) When the Full Moon is in exaltation, own house or Vargas of friendly planets aspected by benefics and free from malefic aspect or conjunction.

(d) When Jupiter is in a Kendra in great strength.

(e) When the Lagna lord is strong in a Kendra or Trikona.

(f) When planets are in exaltation or own signs.

Chart 49 is of a Gandhian whose life extended beyond 95 years. The Moon is afflicted in the 3rd by Ketu. The Ascendant lord Mercury is in the worst Dustana. No benefics occupy Kendras. Only malefics are in

Trikonas. These are Balarishta factors but are neutralised by as many as 3 planets — Jupiter, Saturn and Mars being exalted and the Moon being Full. Additionally and equally effective in putting off early or premature death

Chart 49 : Born 29-2-1896 at 13-00 (LMT) at 20 N 36, 72 N 59 with a balance of 9 days of Venus Dasa at birth.

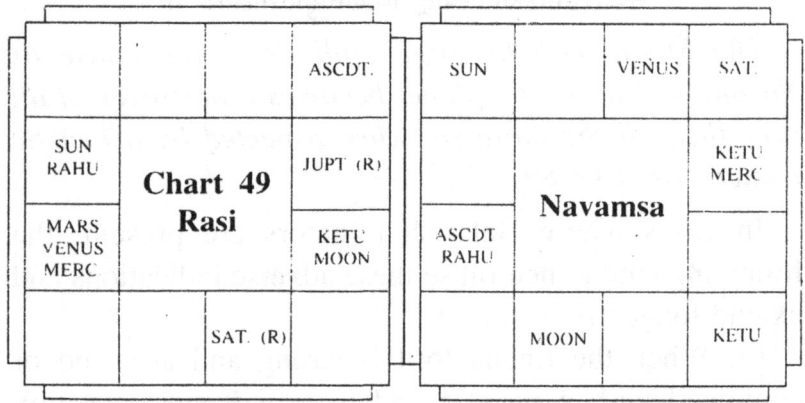

is the fact, the Lagna lord Mercury is in the 8th from Lagna, which though a Dustana, is also the house of longevity and benefits from the Lagna lord's presence in it.

(g) When Rahu is in the 3rd, 6th or the 11th from the Ascendant aspected by benefic planets.

(h) When Rahu is in the Ascendant of Aries, Taurus or Cancer.

(i) When the lord of the sign occupied by the Moon is in the Lagna aspected by benefics.

(j) When the Moon in exaltation is aspected by Venus.

(k) When the birth is in the bright fortnight during night or when the birth is in the dark half during the day, the Moon, even if in the 6th, 7th or the 12th, is aspected both by a benefic and a malefic.

Throughout classical literature on Balarishta Yogas, there is a clause saying the conduct, obviously untoward, of the parents can aggrevate the Dosha. For instance, according to **Phaladeepika** (XIII-3) : मात्रा च पित्रा कृतपापकर्मणा बालग्रहैर्नाशमुपैति बालका:।

These lines are a constant reminder to all parents of the importance of right living in thought, word and deed. They also draw attention to the fact and bring into sharp focus, their own role, overt or inadvertent, in the repercussions their conduct and thoughtless action in contravention of ethical principles can generate on their progeny. Astrology is not only a science but a philosophy of life. It shows trends that await one's progeny during the childhood period and also ways and means to alter them by the subtle yet strong moral and spiritual forces of one's own conduct in life.

Remedial measures are also prescribed in order to overcome the Dosha and its adverse impact. (*ibid, XIII-5*)

तद्दोषशान्त्यै प्रतिजन्मनंतारमाद्वादशाब्दं जपहोमपूर्वकम् ।
आयुष्करं कर्म विधाय ततो बालं चिकित्सादिभिरेव रक्षेत् ॥

In order to offset the Dosha, remedial measures in the form of prescribed Japas and Homas are to be performed on every birthday of the child till its 12th year. These measures must be supplemented with suitable and necessary Chikitsas or medical treatment and thereby, the life of the child is to be protected and promoted.

Chart 48 is an excellent illustration of Balarishta Yoga. Such a chart could have benefited from a prior knowledge of its deficiency in terms of longevity. Suitable remedial measures, as prescribed in **Brihat Parasara Hora** and other classical texts, if performed every year starting from birth, could have shielded the boy protecting him form what befell him. Secondly, the parents could have opted for another child after the boy. Apparently, they presumed, like all parents everywhere in the world do, the boy would have a long healthy life and thereby, did nothing to resist the tragedy that overtook them.

Longevity, apart from Balarishta, is divided into 3 main categories of Alpayu (8 to 32 years), Madhyayu (32 to 75 years) and Poornayu (75 years and above). Different works give slightly differing figures for when Madhyayu ends and Poornayu begins but generally the difference is not beyond 5 years, usually stretching from 70 to 75 years for the change-over from one category to the next.

Chapter 17

**Judging Ayurdaya —
More Guidelines**

LONGEVITY IS closely tied up with the strength of the Ascendant which rules Thanu (तनु) or the physical body. Afflictions to the Ascendant directly or indirectly render its strength to withstand collapse or death fragile and therefore adversely affect the longevity.

The following combinations show medium life :

When the 8th lord is in a Kendra in a fixed sign and the 8th house has no benefics, it shows a 40 year span.

When the 8th lord occupies a Kendra, Mars is in the Lagna and the Sun and Saturn occupy the 3rd and 6th, it shows 44 years.

When the Moon in the Ascendant is Vargottama and is aspected by a malefic or any weak benefics, it shows 48 years.

If the Lagna lord is in a Navamsa ruled by the 8th lord and the 8th lord is in a Navamsa ruled by the Lagna lord, it shows 50 years.

If the Ascendant is a common sign and occupied by Saturn with the Moon in the 8th or the 12th, 33 years longevity is shown.

If all the malefics occupy the 6th, 8th and 12th houses from the Lagna lord and the benefics be in houses other than the 8th, it gives 60 years.

If the Lagna lord and the Moon-sign lord join the 8th lord and Jupiter be in any house, except the Lagna or a Kendra, it shows 65 years.

In all these circumstances, experience has shown the exact figure given for the particular combination is not to be taken as final. What can be taken as final is the upper limit of 65 years depending upon other planetary factors.

The Ascendant receives greatest strength when it is directly influenced by its ruler which is possible when its lord occupies it or aspects it powerfully.

Chart 50 : Born 25-12-1908 at 13h. (GMT) at 51 N 22, 0 W 10 with a balance of 2 months 29 days of Sun Dasa at birth.

SAT.	ASCDT. 19-17		RAHU	MOON		KETU	MERC.
	Chart 50 Rasi				**Navamsa**		MERC. SUN
MOON			JUPT.				
KETU MERC. SUN	VENUS	MARS 28-32			RAHU JUPT.	SAT. VENUS	ASCDT.

Chart 50 is of a cult personality from the show world who died on November 21, 1999 at the age of 91 years. Death beyond 90 years undoubtedly is Purnayu in the strongest sense of the term. The Lagna is Aries powerfully aspected by its ruler Mars from the 7th house. The 7th house aspect is described as the full aspect or the strongest aspect. In this particular case, the planet involved is a natural malefic Mars but who becomes a first-rate functional benefic by virtue of being the Ascendant lord.

The Moon, a very important factor, in assessing longevity, is in the 10th house, the best Kendra, aspected by the Lagna lord.

Chart 51 is of a man who died on May 31, 2000 when 93 years old following a short illness.

The rising sign is Aquarius occupied by its lord Saturn. Saturn is a natural malefic but here he becomes a first-rate benefic being the Ascendant lord. His occupation of Lagna Kendra in his Moolatrikona sign is an added bonus.

Chart 51: Born 7-9-1906 at 6-00 p.m. (EST) at 42 N 19, 72 W 38 with a balance of 7 years 10 months 26 days of Venus Dasa at birth.

	MOON		JUPT	ASCDT	SAT.	MARS	MERC. KETU
ASCDT. 18-38 SAT. (R) 20-19	Chart 51 Rasi		RAHU	JUPT.	Navamsa		
KETU			SUN MARS MERC.				
		VENUS		RAHU VENUS		MOON SUN	

The Moon is in the 3rd aspected by Lagna lord Saturn and Yogakaraka benefic Venus.

Chart 52 is of a famous author known for her romantic novels who died on May 21, 2000 when 100 years old.

Here, the Ascendant Aries is aspected by its lord Mars. The aspect is the adverse 8th house aspect, but it has not affected longevity and has only played a benefic role in promoting Ayus.

The Moon too is in Aries and is aspected by sign-dispositor Mars and benefic Jupiter (R). Ketu is with the Moon. Ketu is in the Ascendant. Is it an affliction that could work against longevity? Normally, though the

Chart 52: Born 9-7-1901 at 11-40 p.m. (GMT) at 52 N 30, 03 W 50 with a balance of 3 years 2 months 29 days of Ketu Dasa at birth.

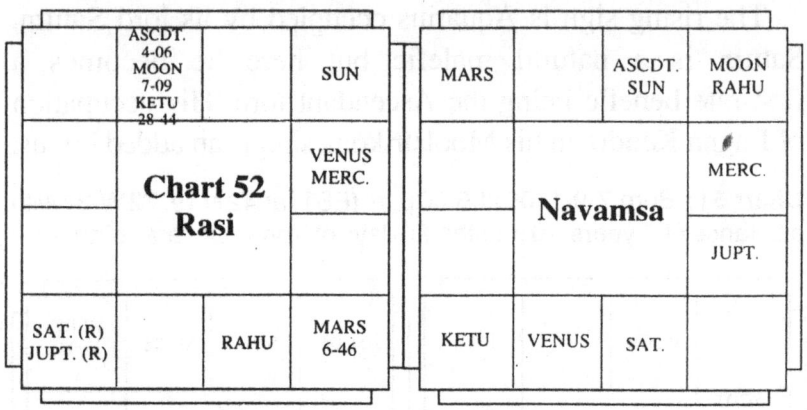

Nodal points are taken to be malefic, Ketu here does not come under any such adverse tag. Ketu is said to give the results of Mars (*Kujavad Ketu*) and Mars is the Lagna lord. Additionally, Ketu benefits from occupying a Martian sign and therefore acting as Mars, a second time over. Ketu in this particular case becomes equivalent to Mars

Chart 53: Born 3-11-1618 at 1-43 p.m. (LMT) at 28 N 39, 77 E 13 with a balance of 2 years 1 month 20 days of Sun Dasa at birth.

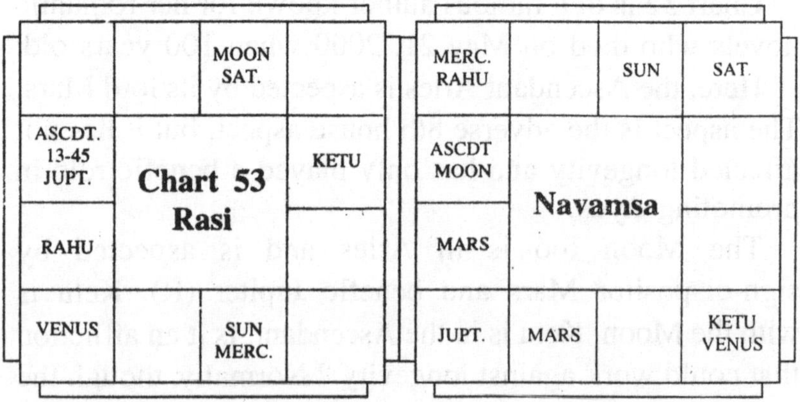

and strengthens the Ayurbhava by his position in the Ascendant.

The Ascendant occupied or aspected by its lord, and the Moon well-placed free of afflictions confers a long life.

Chart 53 is of Emperor Aurangazeb who died in 1707 when 89 years old.

The Ascendant is aspected by its ruler Saturn from the 4th house, a Kendra. The Ascendant Aquarius is Vargottama and thereby, further strengthened.

The Moon is exalted in the 4th house joined by Lagna lord Saturn and free of affliction.

In all these four charts, the common factor is the strength of the Ascendant derived primarily from the influence on it by its ruler by either aspect or occupation. The fact such a planet is a natural malefic makes no difference.

These charts show 2 important factors that ensure good longevity.

1. The Ascendant rendered strong with its ruler aspecting or occupying it, the Vargottama position of the Ascendant or of the Ascendant lord adding to its strength.

2. The Moon in a Kendra (except the 7th) or trine (Trikona) or any other house free from affliction. The Moon should not be in a Dustana — the 6th, 8th or 12th. The 7th house position of the Moon does not help longevity.

When a native is critically ill or seriously injured in an accident or attack, no matter how precarious his condition, such planetary factors as seen so far, give hope of survival and recovery. The physical body, irrespective of the degree and nature of injury it has received or illness it is struck with, will have the wherewithal to draw from hidden reserves of strength and healing to tide over the crisis and return to normalcy.

The two prime factors of a strong Ascendant and the Moon not only take longevity into the Poornayu range but can even extend it to at least 85 years.

The Ascendant lord in Kendras or Trikonas but being so placed as not to aspect the Ascendant directly, gives good longevity, but somewhat less than when there is an aspect on or occupation of the lord in the Ascendant. This could be in the range of 75 to 85 years. But the Moon factor should remain as before, if the longevity should not be reduced.

In the case of a native in his forties who met with a severe road accident, the worried father was assured the native had good Ayus or longevity because of the Lagna lord Venus being in a Kendra in the 4th house with Digbala. Twice, while in hospital, the condition became so critical that even the doctors despaired. But each time the strength of the Ascendant helped the native turn the corner.

Benefics in the 1st, 2nd, 4th, 5th, 7th, 8th, 9th, 10th and 11th houses and malefics in the 3rd, 6th and 11th give good longevity. Likewise, the Sun in a daybirth or the unafflicted Moon for a nightbirth in the 11th ensures good longevity. Saturn, the Karaka or natural significator of Ayus, in the Ayurbhava or the 8th house is a good asset for long life.

The Ascendant lord in the 2nd, 3rd and 11th can give reasonably good longevity but somewhere in the range of 65 to 75 years.

The Ascendant lord in the 12th weakens longevity and brings it into the Madhyayu category. Such natives may *rarely cross 65 years*. Affliction to the Moon can further curtail the life span.

The Ascendant lord in Dustanas rarely gives a life span beyond 60 years. Malefics in Kendras further reduce longevity. But benefics in Kendras help stretch longevity beyond 60 years in such cases.

The Ascendant lord in the 12th is a weakening factor as the 12th is the Kshayastana and affects longevity, but if he is in the 3rd, it is better. In the 6th, the Upachaya effect predominates over the Dustana in reckoning longevity and is therefore, not too bad. But the limit is not beyond Madhyayu.

The Lagna lord in the 8th strengthens the 8th or Ayurbhava on the principle the Ascendant lord promotes the significations of the house he occupies. The 8th house is the Ayurbhava which rules longevity.

The Ascendant lord Venus in Chart 54 though in the 8th, the worst Dustana, is welcome as regards longevity

Chart 54 : Born 12-2-1856 at 12-21 p.m. (LMT) at 18 N, 84 E with a balance of 12 years 3 months 9 days of Venus Dasa at birth.

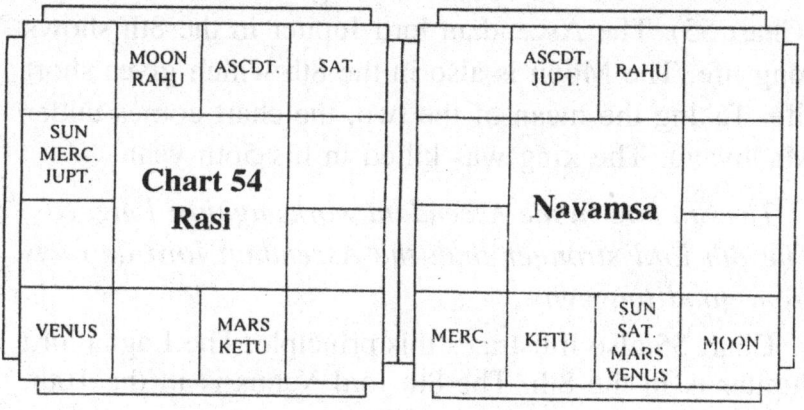

by virtue of his Lagna lordship. Mercury and Jupiter are two benefics in the best Kendra. the 10th.

There are no malefics in Kendras.

The Moon in the 12th works against longevity. But then being aspected by sign-dispositor Mars balances the weakness. Rahu with the Moon is not welcome but as Rahu is said to reflect the results of his sign-dispositor, he acts more like Mars. Rahu is also aspected by Mars, his sign-dispositor, and tends to highlight the Martian influence on the Moon as that of the lunar sign-dispositor and strengthens the Moon thereby.

The Ascendant lord in the 8th can give Poornayu. The Moon in the 8th gives Alpayu. What happens when both the Ascendant lord and the Moon are in the 8th ? In such cases, both factors become active and result in giving Madhyayu. The same is true when the Moon is in the 7th and the Lagna lord in the 8th. Likewise, when the Moon is in the 8th and the Lagna lord is in the 7th (aspecting Lagna), longevity may extend to Madhyayu.

A typical example of the Lagna lord and the Moon in the 8th house is of the late King Birendra of Nepal (Chart 55). The Ascendant lord Jupiter in the 8th shows long life. The Moon is also in the 8th which gives short life. Taking the mean of the two, the chart comes under Madhyayu. The king was killed in his 56th year.

The 8th lord in the Ascendant works against longevity. The 8th lord stronger than the Ascendant lord detracts from good longevity.

Chart 55 also illustrates this principle. The Lagna lord Jupiter is in the 8th. The 8th lord Venus is in the 10th.

Venus as 8th lord gains in strength due to Parivatana with the Lagna lord Jupiter. Jupiter, as a result of his exchange with functional malefic Venus, loses strength. That makes the 8th lord stronger than the Ascendant lord which results in loss to longevity or reduced longevity.

Chart 55: Born 28-12-1945 at 12-00 (ZST) at 27 N 42, 85 E 19 with a balance of 6 months 12 days of Mars Dasa at birth.

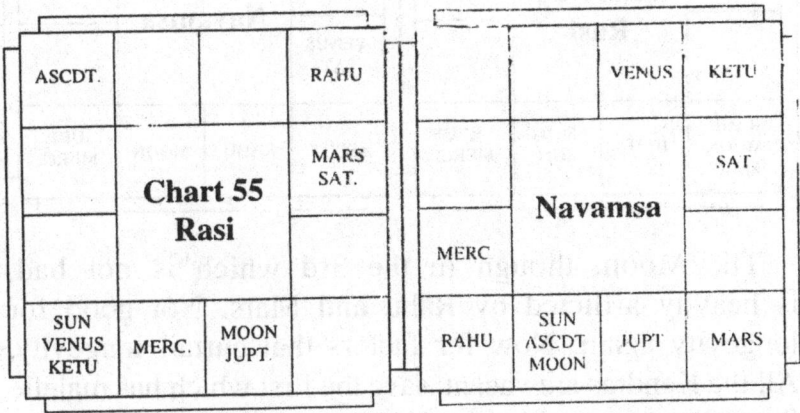

Malefics in Kendras reduce life drastically most times bringing it under Alpayu. If benefics also are in Kendras, then it may be Madhyayu. As always, the Moon's position and strength add to or reduce the longevity so obtained. Here, malefics mean Mars, Saturn, Sun, Rahu and Ketu while Venus, Jupiter and well-associated Mercury are benefics. Rahu and Ketu can get transmuted into playing a benefic role *vis-a-vis* longevity depending upon each individual chart.

In contrast to Chart 54, there is Chart 56 where the life span stopped at 28 years and in which all the factors which work against longevity are present while those that promote longevity are conspicuous by their absence.

The Ascendant Libra is neither aspected nor occupied by its ruler which is an important factor for long life.

Chart 56 : Born 1/2-11-1955 at 5-40 a.m. at 13 N 38, 77 E 23 with a balance of 6 years 1 month 24 days of Venus Dasa.

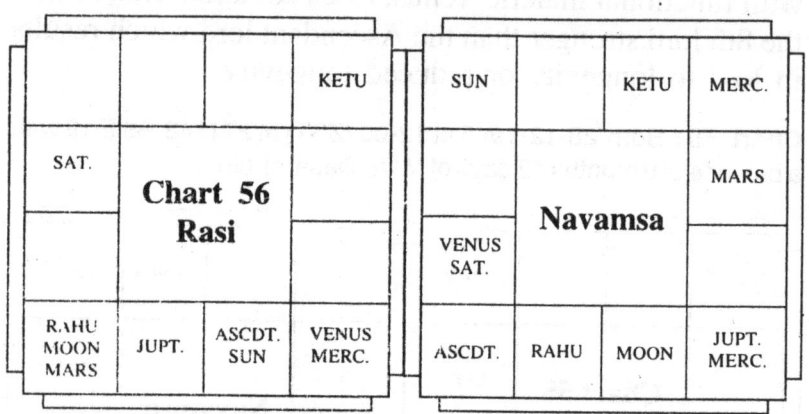

The Moon, though in the 3rd which is not bad, is heavily afflicted by Rahu and Mars. Not good for longevity again. Now for factors that curtail longevity. All the Kendras are vacant, save the first which has malefic Sun. The Ascendant lord is in the 12th. The Ayus, therefore, is drastically reduced to Alpayu. In this chart, Venus is not only the Ascendant lord but also the 8th lord. *The 8th lord if in the 7th (which is the 12th from the 8th), reduces longevity.*

Going back to Chart 50, where 8th lord Mars is in the 7th, Mars here acts primarily as the Ascendant lord. The Moon is well-placed in the 10th and free of affliction. The absence of malefics in Kendras too has helped Mars act more as the Ascendant lord than as a decimated 8th lord in the 12th from the 8th.

Chart 57 is a study in contrast where Lagna lord Venus aspects Lagna but acts more as the 8th lord and whose presence in the 12th from the 8th weakens the 8th house. *This is because the Moon in the 7th damages the longevity potential of a chart* which is further weakened by the presence of malefic Saturn and Ketu in the 4th and Rahu

Chart 57 : Born 6-4-1962 at 8-00 a.m. (IST) at 13 N, 77 E 35 with a balance of 11 years 19 days of Venus Dasa at birth.

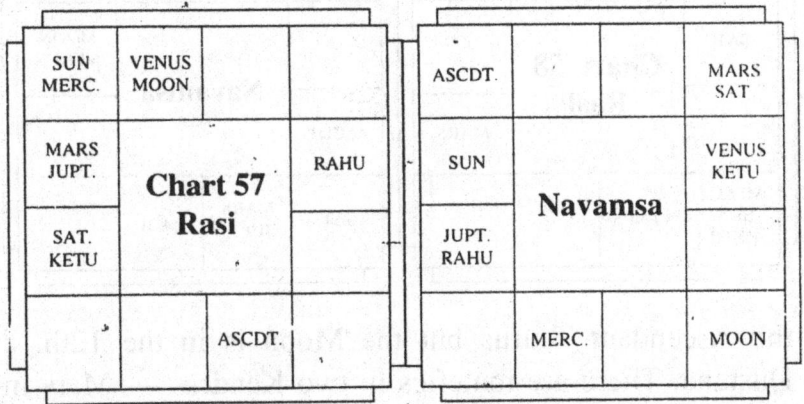

in the 10th, both Kendra houses. The chart suffers from the Moon being in the 7th and the presence of malefics in Kendras. The native died in her 40th year after brain surgery which the doctors described as successful but attributed the death as being due to infection in the site of the surgery.

The 8th lord in the 7th or the 12th adversely effects longevity. Likewise, the 8th lord in a Kendra shortens longevity even if the Lagna lord is in a Kendra, provided the 8th lord is stronger than the Lagna lord.

Swami Vivekananda's chart is another example of the 8th lord Moon in a Kendra in the 10th affecting adversely the longevity given by the Lagna lord by Jupiter in the 11th placing the chart in the Madhyayu category.

In Chart 58, the native died on 12-3-1993 bringing the chart under Alpayu. The Ascendant lord Venus aspects

Chart 58 : Born 15-12-1964 at 18h. at 18 N 58, 72 E 50 with a balance of 1 year 2 months 2 days of Ketu Dasa at birth.

	MOON JUPT.	ASCDT.	RAHU
SAT.	Chart 58 Rasi		
			MARS
MERC. SUN KETU	VENUS		

	SUN KETU		MERC.
	Navamsa		MOON VENUS
ASCDT.			
	SAT.	MARS JUPT.	RAHU

the Ascendant Taurus but the Moon is in the 12th, a Dustana. There are malefics in two Kendras — Mars in the 4th and Saturn in the 10th. The 8th lord Jupiter is in the 12th house from Lagna.

Chapter 18

AYURDAYA
AND CRUCIAL DECISIONS

THE MOON heavily afflicted curtails longevity drastically and brings about death in sudden and unexpected ways.

Chart 59 : Born 30-8-1975 at 8-33 a.m. at 18 N 58, 72 E 50 with a balance of 5 years 7 months 6 days of Moon Dasa at birth.

	JUPT	KETU MOON 15-52 MARS 16-59	
	Chart 59 Rasi		SAT. 6-04
			SUN 14-04 VENUS (R) 9-58
	RAHU		MERC. 7-06 ASCDT. 13-53

MERC.	JUPT	MOON ASCDT.	VENUS (R) MARS
	KETU	**Navamsa**	
			SUN SAT. RAHU

The young native of Chart 59 was an intelligent engineering student in excellent health until April 1994 when he complained of ear-ache followed by fever for about 3 to 4 days. The doctors, on an examination of the lad, said it was blood cancer and treated him with chemotherapy for 4 months. The boy recovered fast and for 3 months carried on in excellent shape. A blood test in January 1995 showed a relapse which the doctors had not expected. On 10-3-1995, the legs became numb, the kidneys were infected and stopped functioning and the boy could not pass urine. He was admitted to the nursing home and put on chemotherapy again for 15 days. Then on 25-3-1995 at about 4-00 a.m. he passed away.

The Ascendant Virgo is occupied by its ruler Mercury which is a good augury for long life. But the benefics Venus and Jupiter are in the 12th and 8th respectively in Dustanas which are Alpayu factors in cases where the Balarishta span has been tided over. The Moon is exalted and Vargottama in a trine in the 9th. Yet, did not help. The Moon is under heavy affliction from Mars who is not only a natural malefic but the baneful 8th lord in this case. The Nodes also afflict the Moon. Ketu acts as Mars and Mars is the adverse 8th lord. Ketu can act as his sign-dispositor Venus too but Venus is in the 12th.

In a middle-aged regional politician's chart where the country has to meet heavy expenditure on Z-category security because of apprehensions of threat to life from secessionist forces, the fact the 7th and 10th Kendras have powerful natural benefics, Rahu is in the 11th house and the Lagna lord Mercury is in a trine together with the fact, the Moon is full in the 3rd house is guarantee enough there could be no danger to life from any source, the chart coming under Poornayu. But the same cannot be said of another politician with similar security arrangements. This person has the Lagna lord in the 12th though with digital strength while 8th lord Saturn occupies Lagna. These bring the chart under the Madhyayu group and expose the native to danger of violence. The security provided to this leader appears to be astrologically justified for longevity can indeed come under threat.

In May 1993, the native of Chart 60, who was in perfect health, was persuaded by a close friend, a noted cardiologist, to go through a series of tests on medical equipment and machines imported from England and newly installed in his consulting rooms. The tests revealed frightening symptoms of a heart condition requiring immediate surgery. The cardiologist was deeply concerned for his friend and advised him that a by-pass surgery be gone through at once as otherwise there was danger of a fatal attack any moment.

Chart 60 : Born 28-11-1939 at 9-00 a.m. (IST) at 13 N 01, 78 E 10 with a balance of 4 years 1 month 7 days of Mars Dasa at birth.

JUPT. MANDI	SAT. (R) KETU	MOON				KETU VENUS SAT. (R)	
MARS	\multicolumn{2}{c}{Chart 60 Rasi}		MARS	\multicolumn{2}{c}{Navamsa}	
	\multicolumn{2}{c}{XVI - 160/93}					
ASCDT VENUS	SUN MERC. (R)	RAHU			SUN MERC. (R) RAHU		ASCDT. MOON JUPT. MANDI

The native was confused. He was even alarmed by the reports. The cardiologist meanwhile sent the reports to the All India Institute of Medical Sciences at Delhi for expert opinion which only confirmed his worst fears. Harried and excited, the two friends sought an astrological assessment before a final decision on whether to go in for surgery.

The rising sign Sagittarius is a powerful sign and is occupied by natural benefic Venus. The Lagna lord Jupiter is in his own sign Pisces, in the 4th, a Kendra. The Moon is full and exalted. Rahu occupies the 11th. These four factors were highlighted as contributing to a long life that could easily place the chart in the Poornayu group with a longevity of at least 75 years.

The native was in his 54th year at that time. Therefore, astrologically it was quite clear there was no immediate threat or danger to life as indicated by the medical tests. Secondly, the Lagna lord in strength and the Karaka for the heart, the Sun, Vargottama ruled out the serious heart condition diagnosed with the aid of high-tech instruments. The two friends felt sufficiently convinced by the astrological diagnosis to decide against the surgery. In 2001, the native continues to be alive and kicking and the massive heart attack, feared any moment by the medical specialists, has still not struck.

In yet another case of a similar nature, the native of Chart 61 who was in excellent shape, was invited to undergo a series of complimentary tests on newly installed medical apparatus at a prestigious medical academy in a coastal town in the South by a doctor friend. What was his consternation when the friend rang up to give him the alarming results of the tests — a serious heart condition necessitating immediate surgery. This was in 1989.

Chart 61 has Virgo rising with Jupiter in a Kendra as also Venus, both benefics. The Lagna lord Mercury in the 8th is good for longevity. The Moon is in the 10th. These are the plus factors against which there are malefic Mars and Rahu also in the 10th. Nevertheless, Jupiter in the 7th aspecting the Ascendant and the Lagna lord in the 8th were indentified along with the Moon in a Kendra as capable of confering long life. In other words, the chances of a fatal attack were dismissed. And of course, though

Chart 61 : Born 5-5-1927 at 3-25 p.m. (IST) at 13 N 23, 74 E 45 with a balance of 7 years 8 months 22 days of Rahu Dasa at birth.

JUPT.	MERC. SUN		VENUS MOON MARS RAHU
	Chart 61 Rasi XI - 244/89		
KETU			ASCDT.

MARS		MERC.	KETU
LAGNA MOON	Navamsa		JUPT.
RAHU	SAT.	SUN VENUS	

not directly relevant to our discussion now, the exalted Sun and benefic influence on the Ascendant were pointed out as shielding heart-health. The native did not go in for surgery though every effort was made by well-meaning medical friends to make him change his mind.

The native continues in good health even in 2001 and the medically diagnosed heart condition appears to have gone into hibernation. Such situations often confuse patients. The question of longevity assessed astrologically can save one not only from the panic such medical advice can cause, but also avoid unnecessary surgery as well as heavy financial drain, considering the fact more than ninety percent of the population is made up of the lower and middle income groups who simply cannot afford such heavy medical bills and all the dislocation the hospitalization and its attendant problems bring in into their lives, and especially when the surgery itself may be quite redundant.

Longevity according to most schools of Indian astrology is not beyond human control. Astrological works repeatedly stress that attitudes and life-style have a great influence on the quality as well as quanta of life one enjoys. No one will dispute the fact that most anti-social elements and gangsters, whose lives are a confusing mix of violence, hate, anger, jealousy, greed, and of course, arrogance, rarely, if ever, cross their forties. In strong contrast, there are countless examples, including those of the respected Ramakrishna Mission, where a life of spirituality, piety, peace and regulation has given spans nearing ninety and even more.

Jataka Parijata aptly sums up the philosophy of Ayurdaya in the following Slokas.

ये धर्मकर्मनिरता द्विजदेवभक्ता ये पथ्यभोजनरता विजितेन्द्रियाश्च।
ये मानवा दधति सत्कुलशीलसीमास्तेषमिदं कथितमायुरुदारधीभि: ॥
V-35

This Ayus has been declared by wise men in respect of those who are engaged in the practice of virtuous actions, who are devoted to the pious and to God, who eat wholesome food, who keep their senses under control and who preserve the noble traditions of character and conduct of their families.

ये पापलुब्धाश्चौरा ये देवब्राह्मणनिन्दका: ।
ब्रह्माशिनश्च ये तेषामकालमरणं नृणाम् ॥ V-36

Premature death overtakes those who are sinful, covetous, thievish, who revile God and the virtuous and who are addicted to gluttony.

धर्मे विकल्पबुद्धिनां दु:शीलानां च विद्विषाम् ।
ब्राह्मणानां च देवानां परद्रव्यापहारिणाम् ॥   V-37

भयंकरणां सर्वेषां मूर्खाणां पिशुनस्य च ।
स्वधर्माचारहीनानां पापकर्मोपजीविनां ॥   V-38

शास्त्रेष्वनियतानां च मूढानामपमृत्यव: ।
अन्येषामुत्तमायु: स्यादिति शास्त्रविदो विदु : ॥ V-39

Sudden death siezes those that are sceptical of the force of moral law, who are vicious and hateful of God and the pious, who steal others' goods, who are a source of dread to all, who are foolish and indulge in calumny, who have abandoned their duties and observances, who live by sinful sources, and those who would not wholly abide by the tenets of the sacred scriptures. Those who excel (in astrology) regard the rules of Ayus as applying only to people other than those declared as liable to untimely death.

All combinations for good longevity come with a rider — faith in God and right living or ethical living.

Nothing illustrates these truths of Ayurdaya in astrology more than the following case (Chart 62).

The Ascendant Scorpio is occupied by its own ruler Mars. Benefics Jupiter and Mercury also occupy it. The Moon is in the 9th in a trine free of afflictions and in his own sign. At the same time, the Moon also has digital strength and benefits from a trinal Jupiterean aspect. The prime longevity factors of a strong Ascendant and the Moon obtain in this chart. And theoretically add up to Poornayus, may be beyond 85 years even. But look at the facts and you will see how remarkably true it is that

	KETU		
	Chart 62 Rasi		MOON
SUN SAT	LAGNA MARS MERC JUPT	VENUS	RAHU

RAHU	VENUS	SUN	
	Navamsa		
			SAT
MERC	MARS JUPT		MOON KETU LAGNA

one can hopelessly mess up the longevity promised in the chart by wrong actions and thoughts.

The native married an attractive woman. Both were earning handsomely and together, this added up to a fabulous six-figure income. The wife got pregnant; the native wanted her to terminate the pregnancy for fear the baby would mean she would have to give up her job and her salary. When she refused to comply with him, the husband hit upon a cruel plan. He began to insure her for huge sums of money. He hoped to enjoy the thousands her insurance policies would bring him after her death. He then shot her dead at point-blank range. He managed to get away with the sob-story that an unknown gunman had killed his dear wife. The case made headlines and public sympathy was with the native who seemed so shattered by his wife's death. No one knew the truth except his younger brother to whom he had divulged it. But guarding the dreadful secret was sheer torture and the brother, after a few months of intense mental agony, reported it to the police. When the police came, the native now knew there was no escape and killed himself by jumping into the water from a bridge.

A careful analysis of the case raises the following questions : Why did the man get so avaricious inspite of earning well ? Why did he set himself unrealistic monetary goals ? Why did he insure his wife and why, for God's sake, did he want the huge insurance sums his wife's death could bring him ? It was only greed all the way. Only if he had not coveted the money, he would not have killed her and if he had not shot her dead, there would have been no reason to dread the police. If he had nothing to panic about, why would he jump to his watery grave ? At every stage, it looks like he could have averted his death and enjoyed the long life which his chart warranted. Money was not the problem. He had enough, but he wanted more. And so he chose to do everything within his power to attract the adverse consequences attributed to such living in astrological works. The following Sloka (**JP** V. 110) clearly brings this case under its purview :

लग्नाष्टमे पापयुतेऽस्टमेशे रि:फोपयते यदि केन्द्रमे वा ।
लग्नेश्वरे हीनबलेन युक्ते दुर्मार्गदोषात्प्रवदन्ति मृत्यु: ॥

meaning,
when a malefic planet occupies the 8th Bhava (Mars aspects the 8th, so do the Sun and Saturn) *and the lord thereof occupies the 12th or a Kendra* (Mercury is in Lagna Kendra) *and the lord of the rising sign is deficient in strength* (Mars is highly malefic, though not exactly deficient in strength in Scorpio), *death is said to result from the evil effects of pursuing a wicked course of life.*

The Sloka does not say when life will end because of certain planetary factors. But it clearly cautions against evil tendencies which, if not reined in and resisted, can lead one to certain and premature death. Even death, which is inevitable, therefore, appears to be well within the scope of free-will. Rather, long life, one can surmise from such cases, is very much within our power and can be harnessed from the planetary combinations in the birth chart. When such is the case, how can any mature intellect charge astrology with fatalism ? *12-2001* •